AUDIO ACCESS INCLUDED
Recorded Piano Accompaniments Online

PLAYBACK+
Speed • Pitch • Balance • Loop

classic standards

Arranged by Brent Edstrom

To access audio visit:
www.halleonard.com/mylibrary

"Enter Code"
3415-1144-2204-2772

ISBN 978-1-5400-4193-7

Visit Hal Leonard Online at
www.halleonard.com

Contact us:
Hal Leonard
7777 West Bluemound Road
Milwaukee, WI 53213
Email: info@halleonard.com

In Europe, contact:
Hal Leonard Europe Limited
42 Wigmore Street
Marylebone, London, W1U 2RN
Email: info@halleonardeurope.com

In Australia, contact:
Hal Leonard Australia Pty. Ltd.
4 Lentara Court
Cheltenham, Victoria, 3192 Australia
Email: info@halleonard.com.au

ARRANGER'S NOTE

The vocalist's part in the *Singer's Jazz Anthology* matches the original sheet music but is *not* intended to be sung verbatim. Instead, melodic embellishments and alterations of rhythm and phrasing should be incorporated to both personalize a performance and conform to the accompaniments. In some cases, the form has been expanded to include "tags" and other endings not found in the original sheet music. In these instances, the term *ad lib.* indicates new melodic material appended to the original form.

Although the concept of personalizing rhythms and embellishing melodies might seem awkward to singers who specialize in classical music, there is a long tradition of melodic variation within the context of performance dating back to the Baroque. Not only do jazz singers personalize a given melody to fit the style of an accompaniment, they also develop a distinctive sound that helps *further* personalize their performances. Undoubtedly, the best strategy for learning how to stylize a jazz melody is to listen to recordings from the vocal jazz canon, including artists such as Nat King Cole, Ella Fitzgerald, Billie Holiday, Frank Sinatra, Sarah Vaughan, Nancy Wilson, and others.

The accompaniments in the *Singer's Jazz Anthology* can also be embellished by personalizing rhythms or dynamics, and chord labels are provided for pianists who are comfortable playing their own chord voicings. In some cases, optional, written-out improvisations are provided. These can be performed "as is," embellished, or skipped, depending on the performers' preference.

The included audio features piano recordings that can be used as a rehearsal aid or to accompany a performance. Tempi were selected to fit the character of each accompaniment, and the optional piano solos were omitted to provide a more seamless singing experience for vocalists who utilize them as backing tracks.

I hope you find many hours of enjoyment exploring the *Singer's Jazz Anthology* series!

Brent Edstrom

All The Things You Are

from VERY WARM FOR MAY

Lyrics by OSCAR HAMMERSTEIN II
Music by JEROME KERN

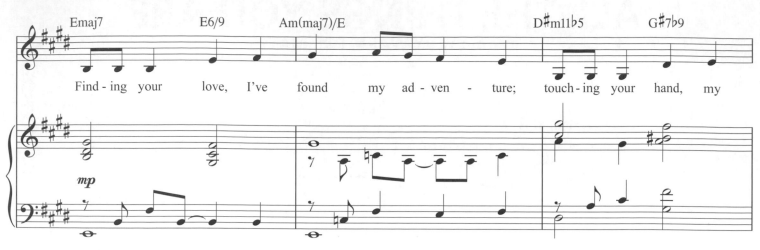

Find-ing your love, I've found my ad-ven - ture; touch-ing your hand, my

heart beats the fast - er. All that I want in all of this world is

Medium Swing

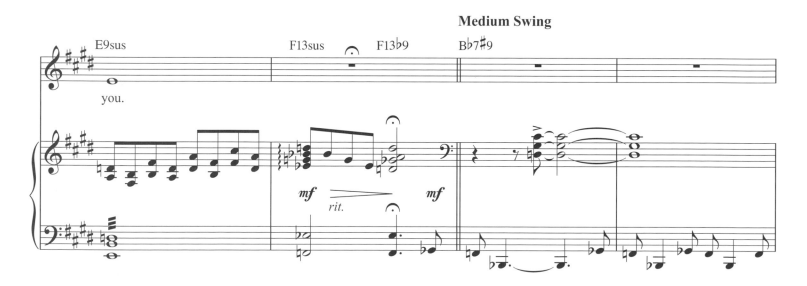

you.

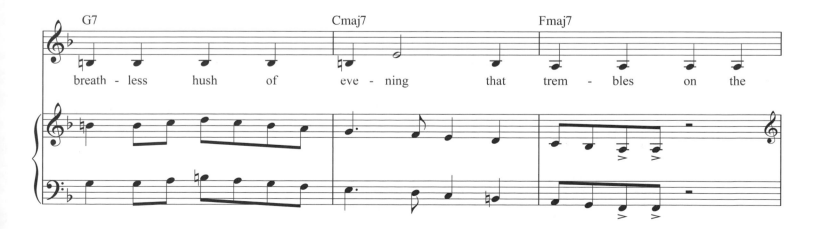

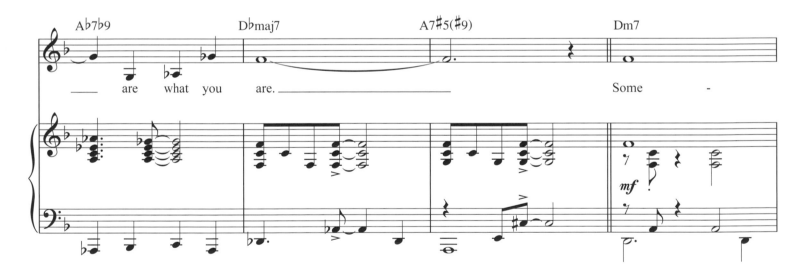

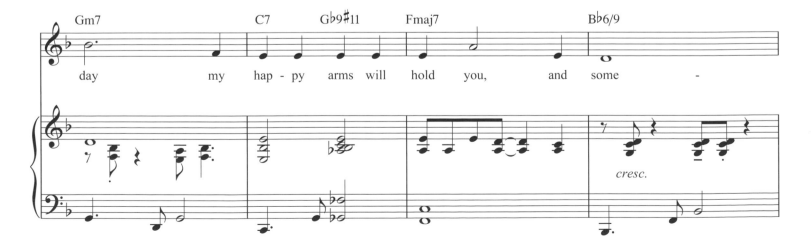

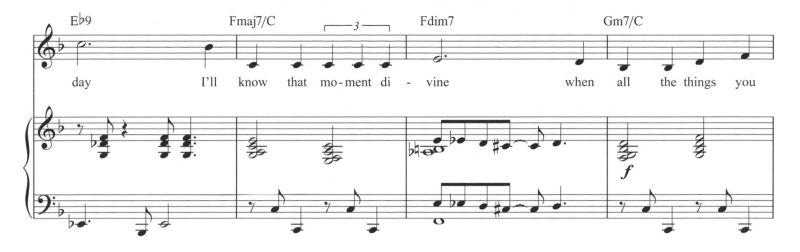

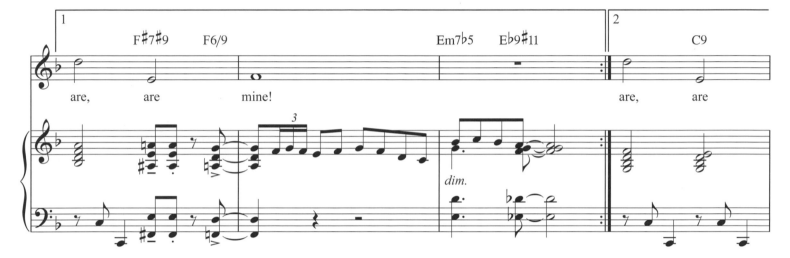

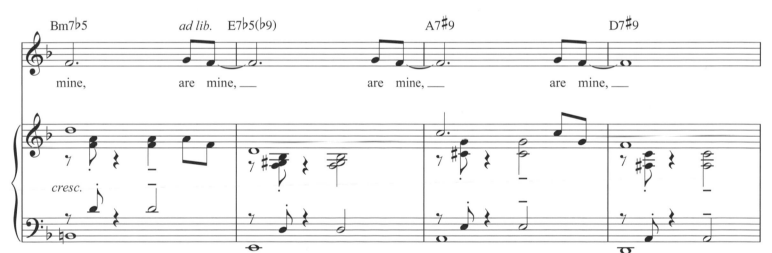

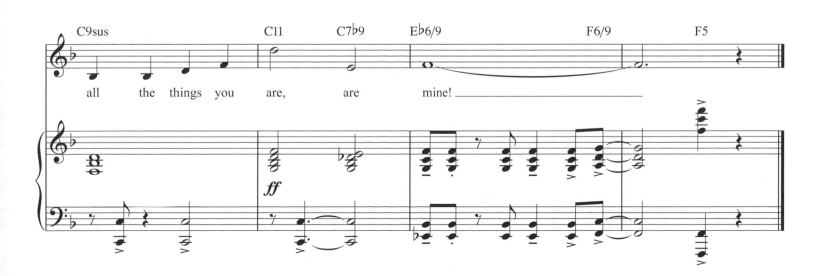

AUTUMN LEAVES

English lyric by JOHNNY MERCER
French lyric by JACQUES PREVERT
Music by JOSEPH KOSMA

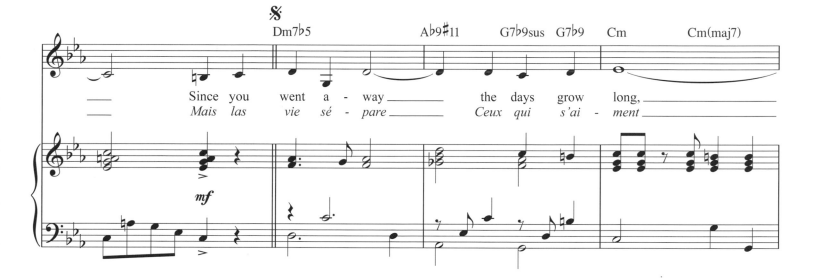

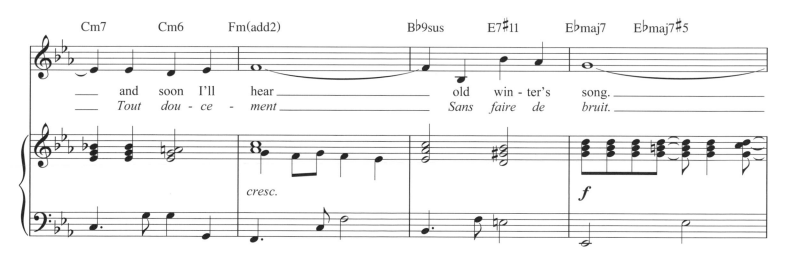

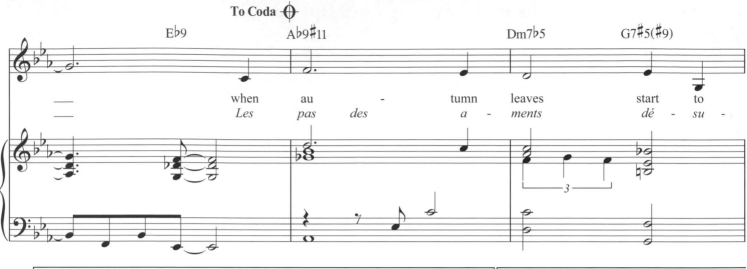

when au - tumn leaves start to
Les pas des a - ments dé - su -

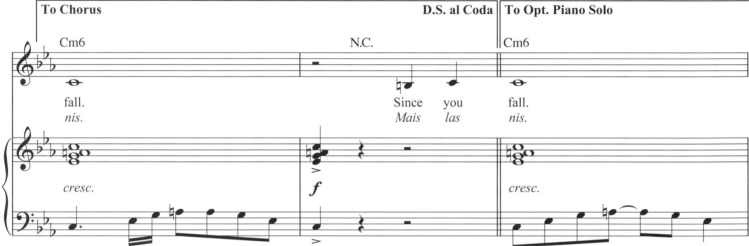

fall.
nis.
Since you fall.
Mais las nis.

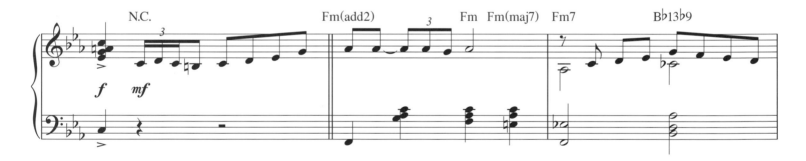

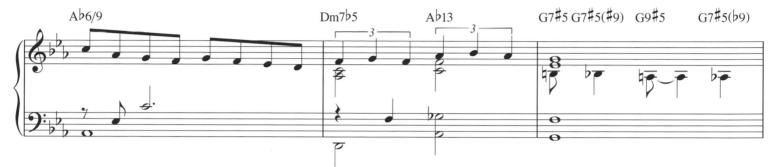

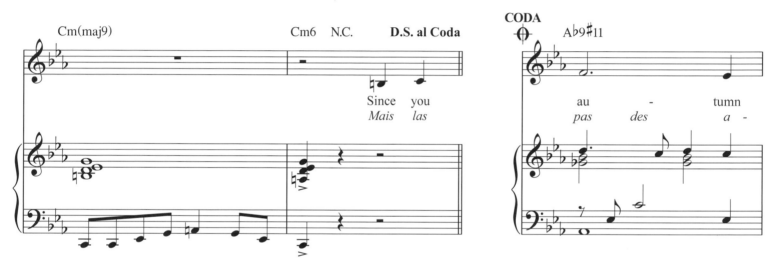

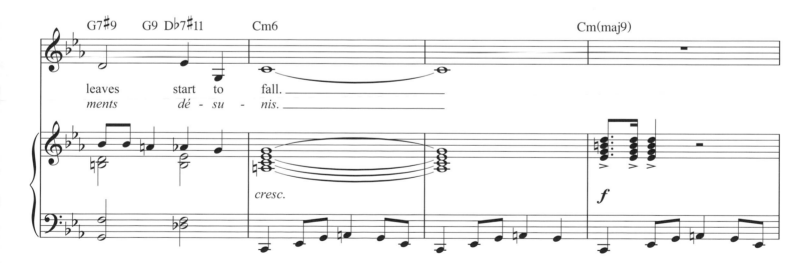

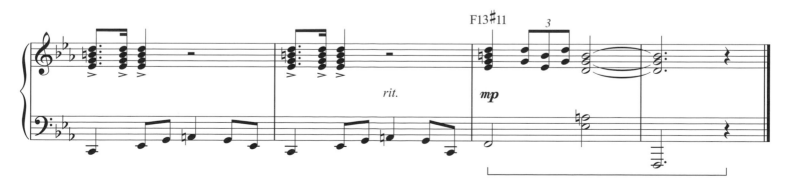

ALMOST LIKE BEING IN LOVE

from BRIGADOON

Lyrics by ALAN JAY LERNER
Music by FREDERICK LOEWE

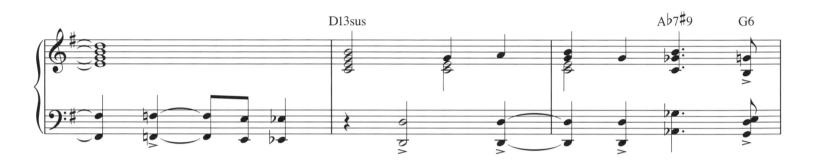

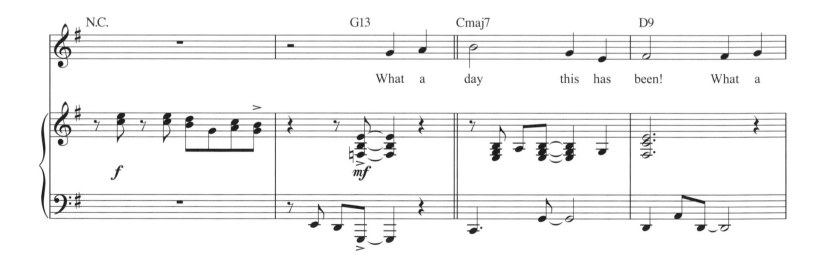

What a day this has been! What a rare mood I'm in! Why, it's al-most like

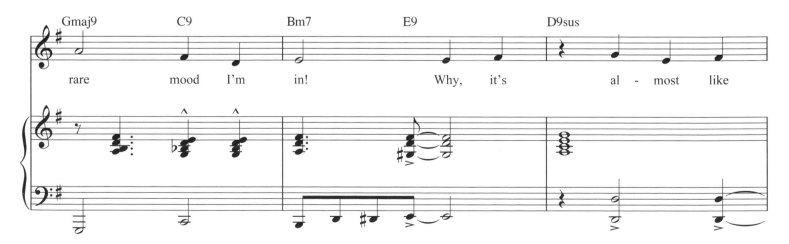

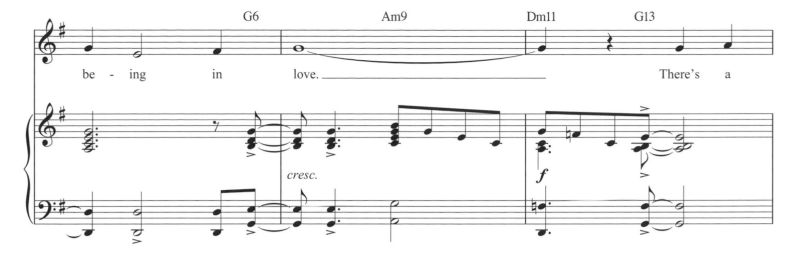

being in love. _____ There's a

smile on my face for the whole hu- man

race. Why, it's al- most like be- ing in love! _____

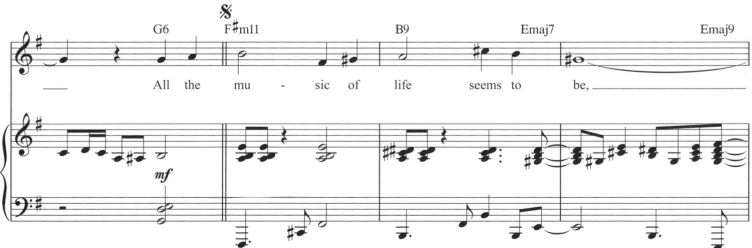

_____ All the mu- sic of life seems to be, _____

To Chorus **D.S. al Coda** | **To Opt. Piano Solo**

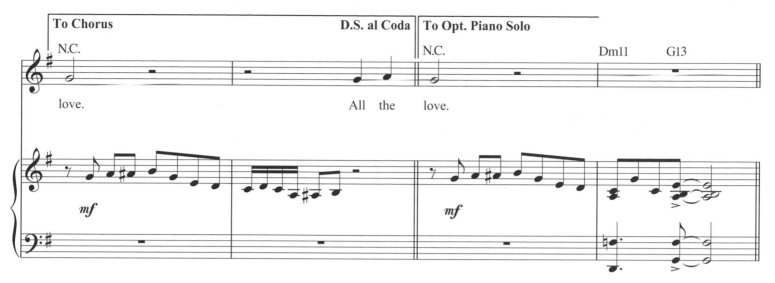

love.   All the love.

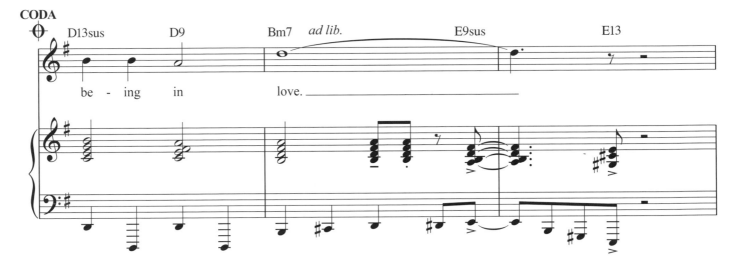

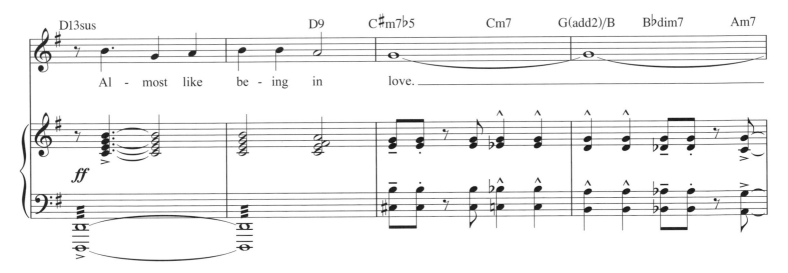

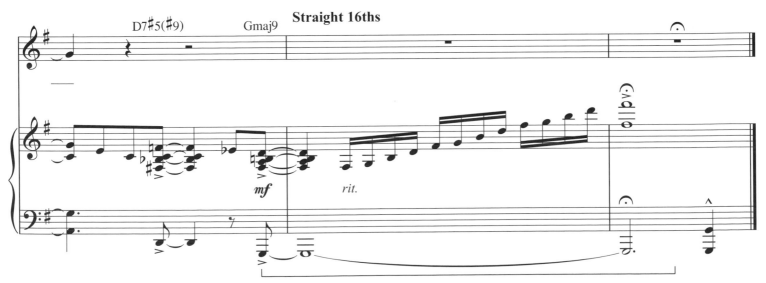

CHEEK TO CHEEK
from the RKO Radio Motion Picture TOP HAT

Words and Music by
IRVING BERLIN

Moderately fast Swing

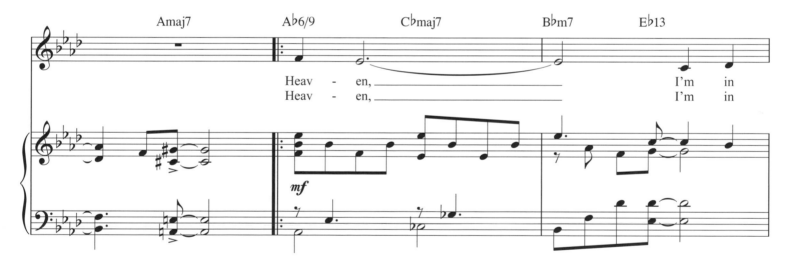

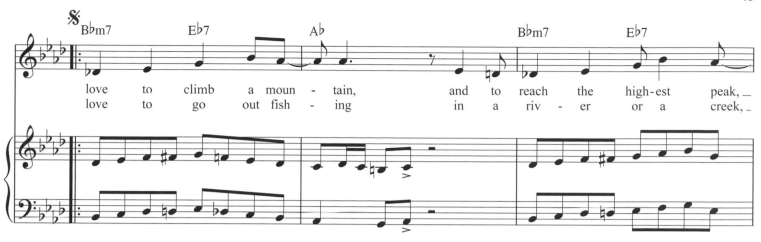

love to climb a moun - tain, and to reach the high-est peak, _
love to go out fish - ing in a riv - er or a creek, _

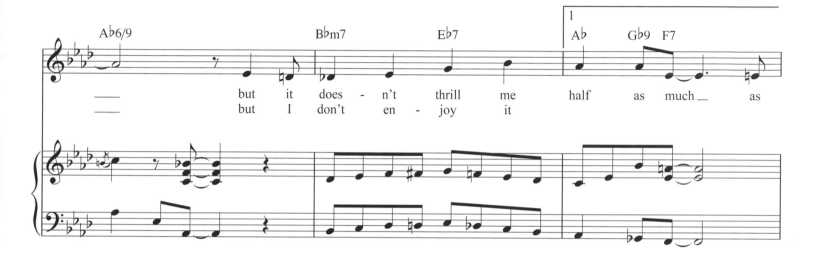

— but it does - n't thrill me half as much _ as
— but I don't en - joy it

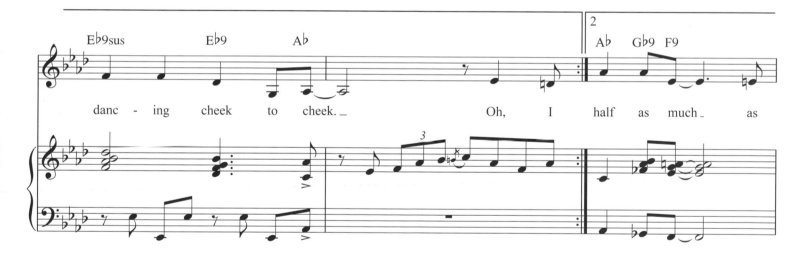

danc - ing cheek to cheek. _ Oh, I half as much _ as

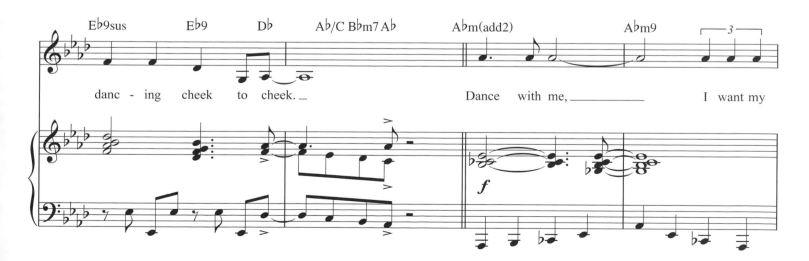

danc - ing cheek to cheek. _ Dance with me, _____ I want my

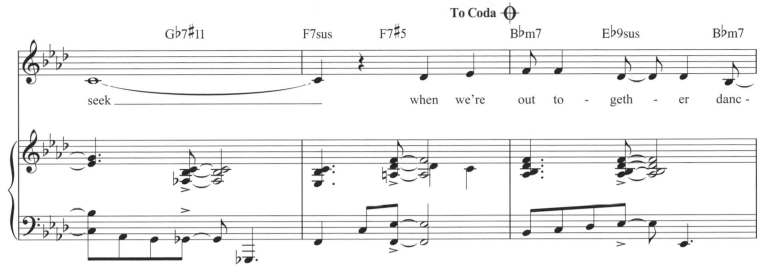

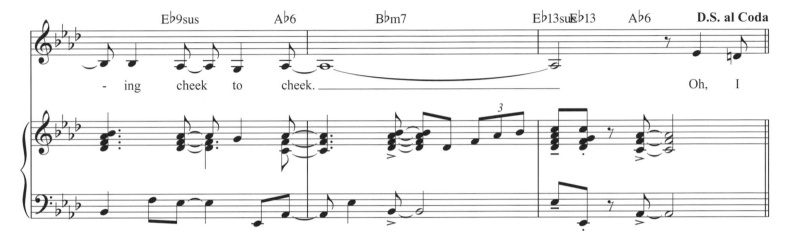

BLUE SKIES
from BETSY

Words and Music by
IRVING BERLIN

Moderate Swing

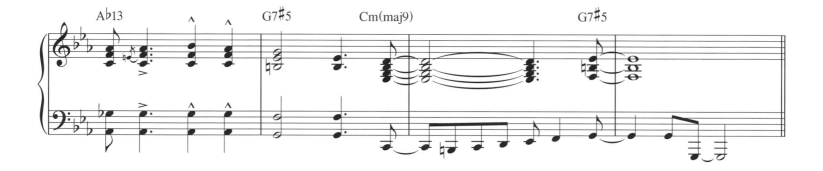

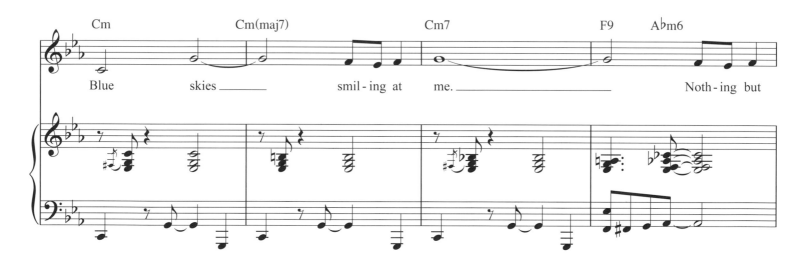

Blue   skies _____ smil-ing at   me. _____   Noth-ing but

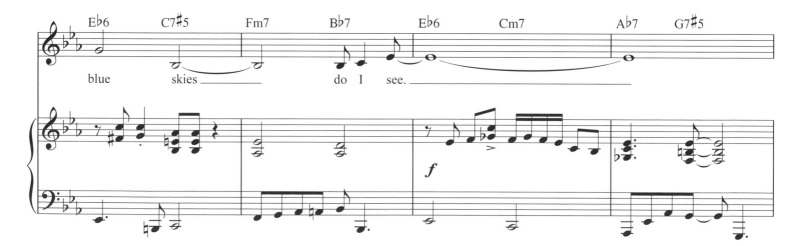

blue   skies _____ do I   see.

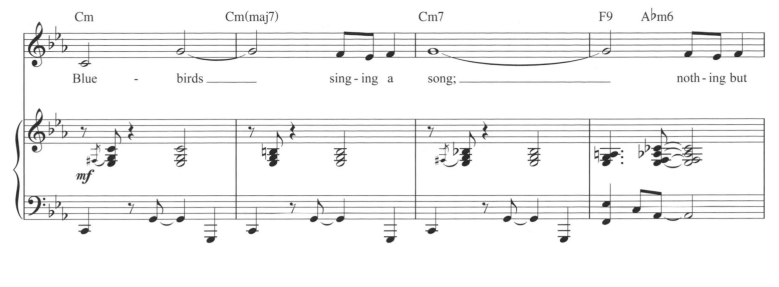

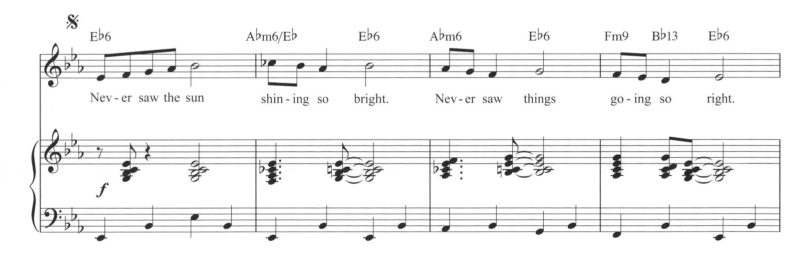

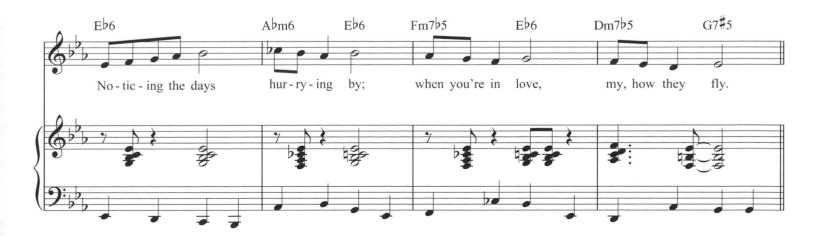

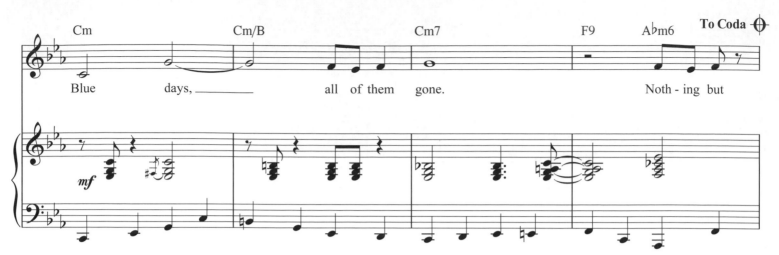

Blue days, _____ all of them gone. Noth - ing but

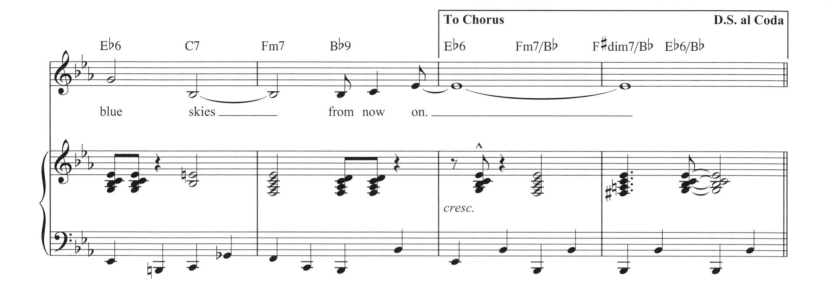

blue skies _____ from now on. _____

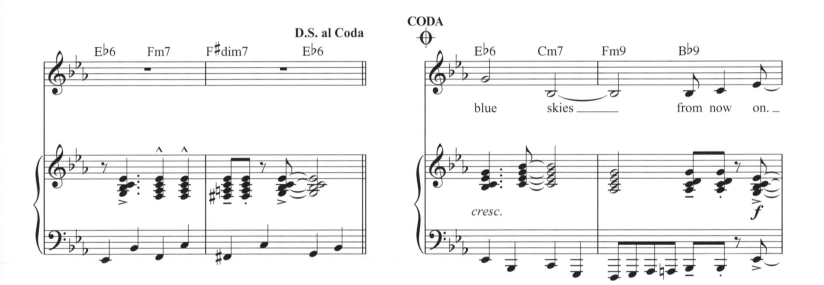

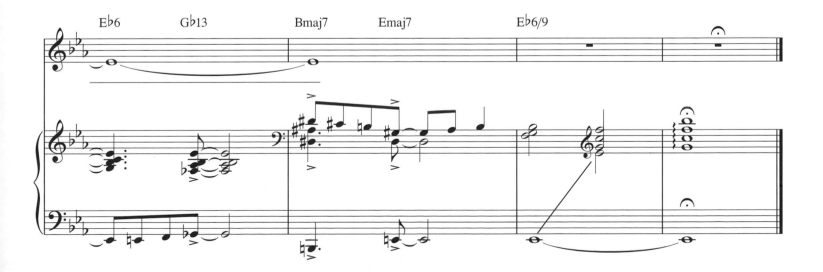

BODY AND SOUL

from THREE'S A CROWD

Words by EDWARD HEYMAN,
ROBERT SOUR and FRANK EYTON
Music by JOHN GREEN

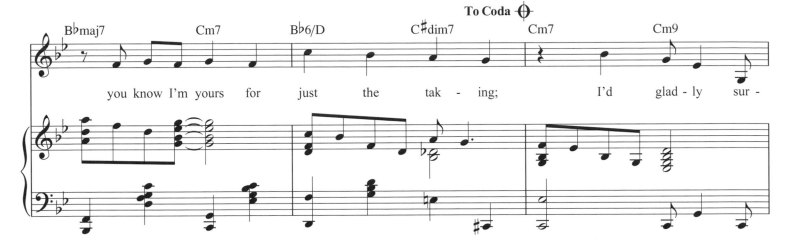

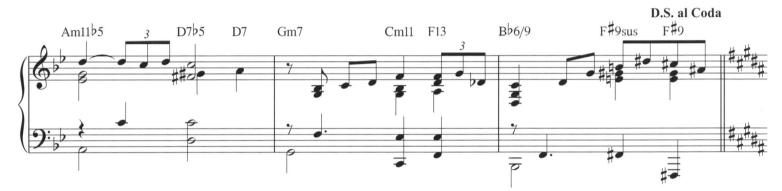

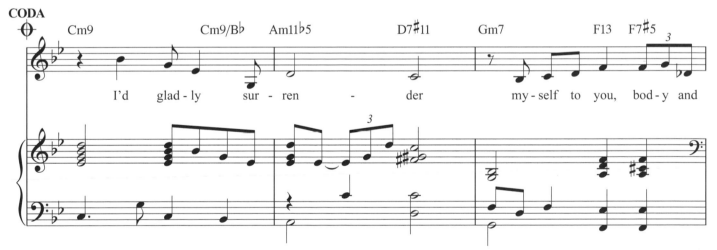

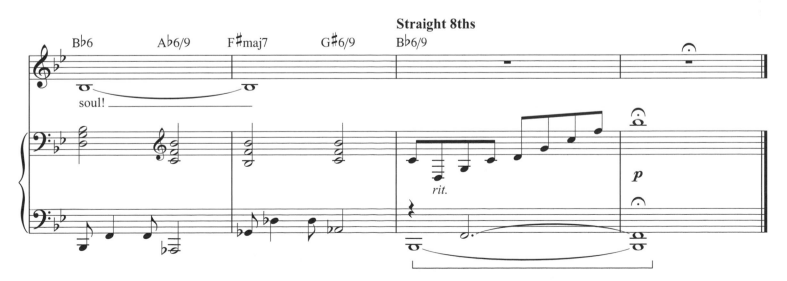

COME RAIN OR COME SHINE

from ST. LOUIS WOMAN

Words by JOHNNY MERCER
Music by HAROLD ARLEN

Slow Swing

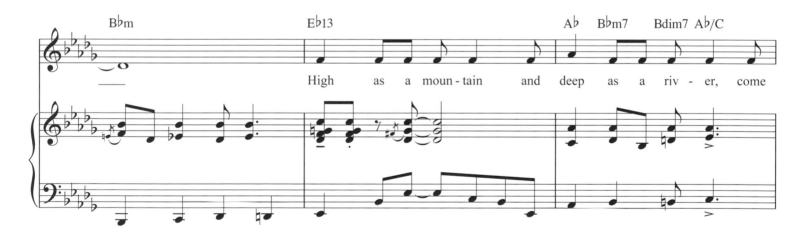

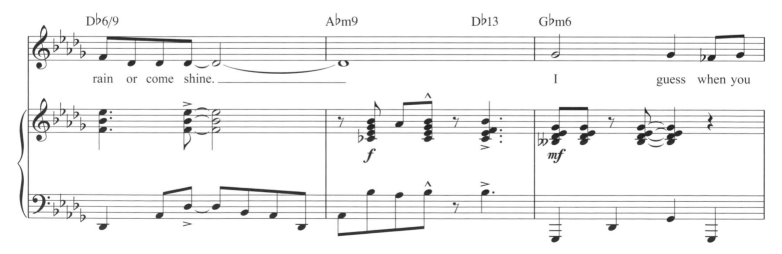

met me it was just one of those things, but don't ev-er bet me 'cause I'm gon-na be true if you let me.

You're gon-na love me like no-bod-y's loved me, come rain or come shine.

Hap-py to-geth-er, un-hap-py to-geth-er, and

won't it be fine? _____ Days may be cloud-y or sun-ny. We're

To Coda ⊕

in or we're out of the mon-ey, but I'm with you al-ways, I'm with you rain __ or

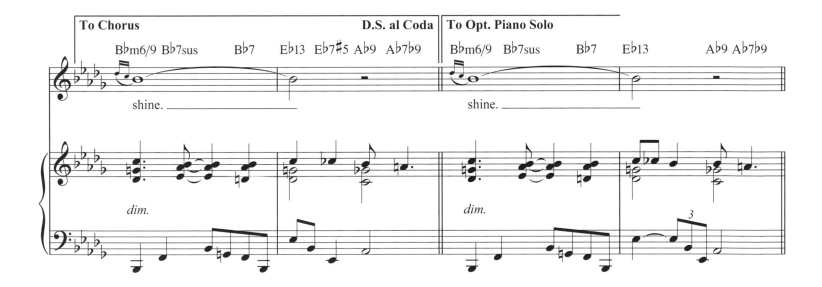

To Chorus   **D.S. al Coda** | **To Opt. Piano Solo**

shine. _____   shine. _____

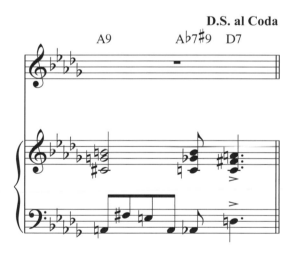

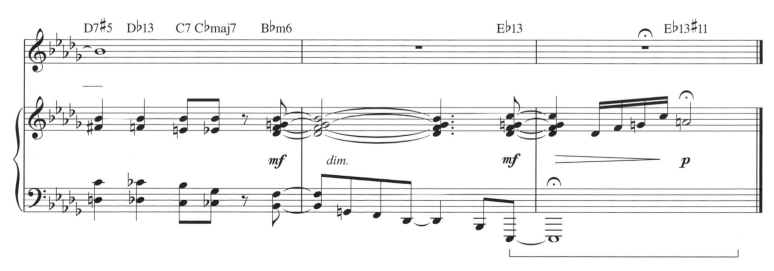

I'm with you rain or shine.

DO NOTHIN' TILL YOU HEAR FROM ME

Words and Music by DUKE ELLINGTON
and BOB RUSSELL

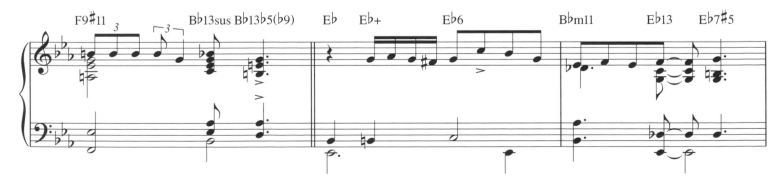

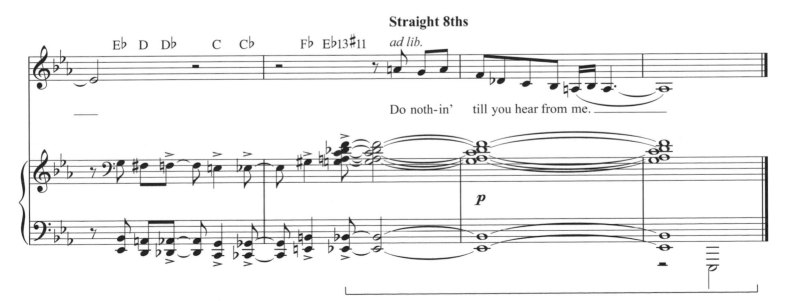

FLY ME TO THE MOON
(In Other Words)
featured in the Motion Picture ONCE AROUND

Words and Music by
BART HOWARD

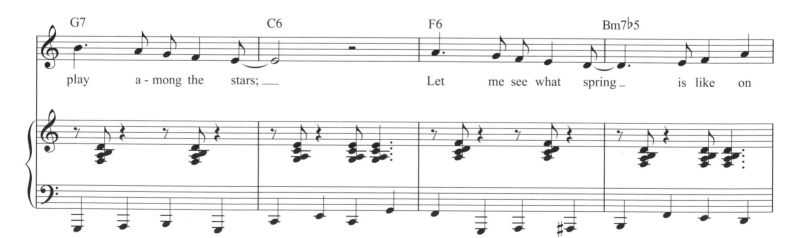

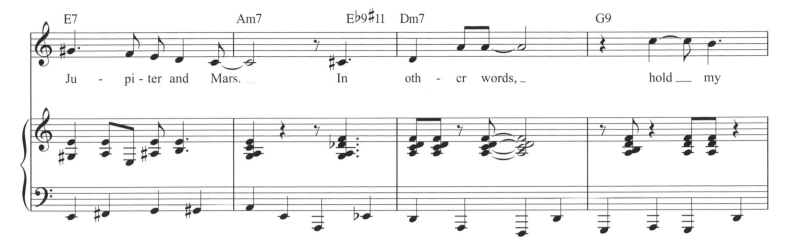

Ju - pi - ter and Mars. In oth - er words, In oth - er words, _ hold _ my

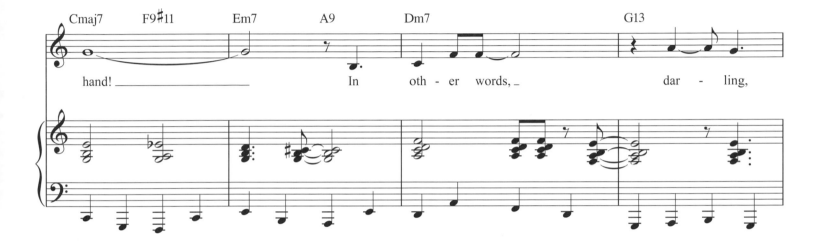

hand! _____ In oth - er words, _ dar - ling,

kiss me! _____ Fill my heart with song, _ and let me

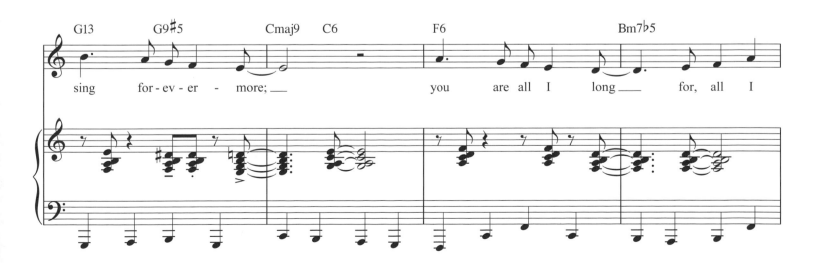

sing for - ev - er - more; _ you are all I long _ for, all I

To Coda

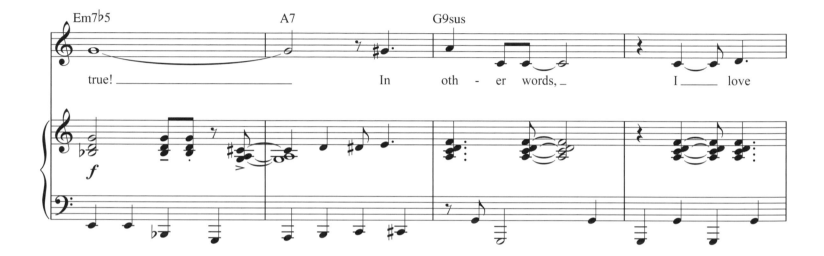

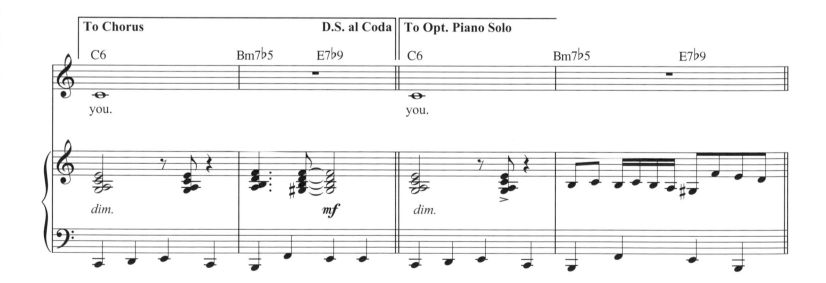

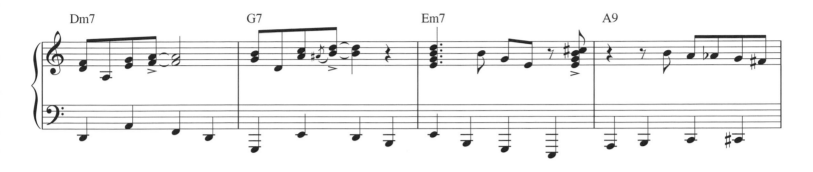

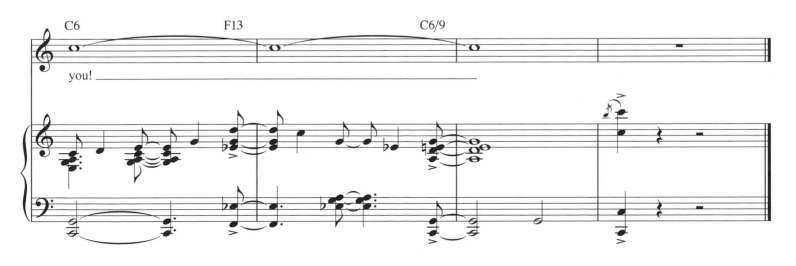

true! _____ In oth-er words, _____ I _____ love

you! _____

GEORGIA ON MY MIND

Words by STUART GORRELL
Music by HOAGY CARMICHAEL

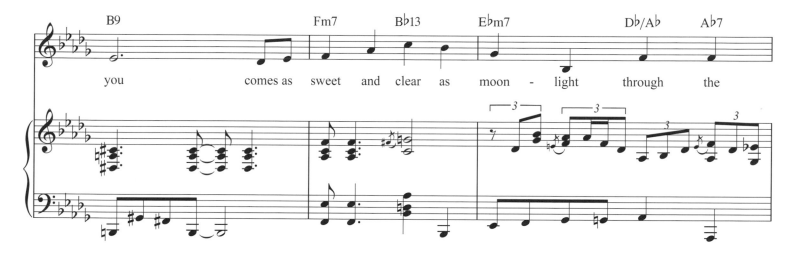

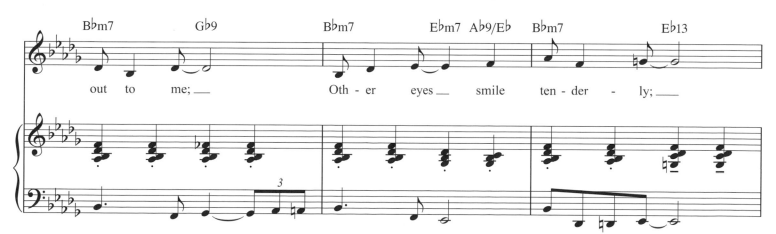

44

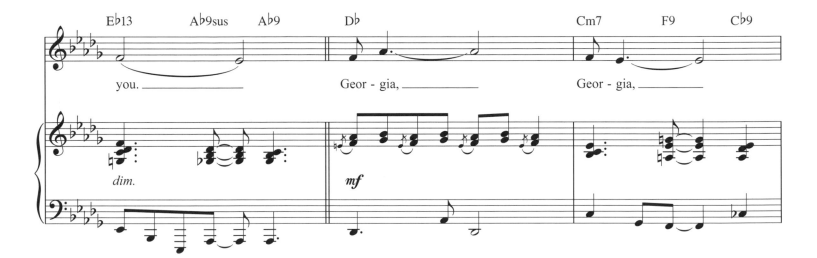

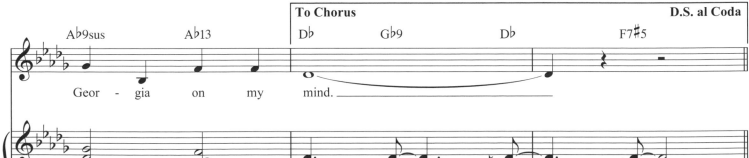

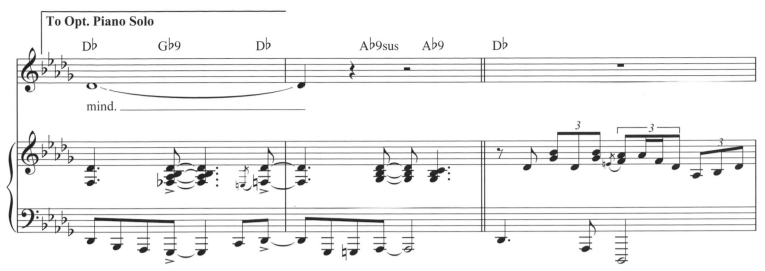

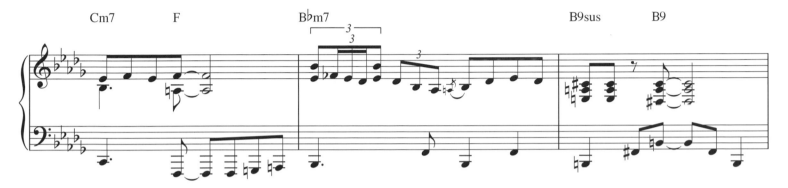

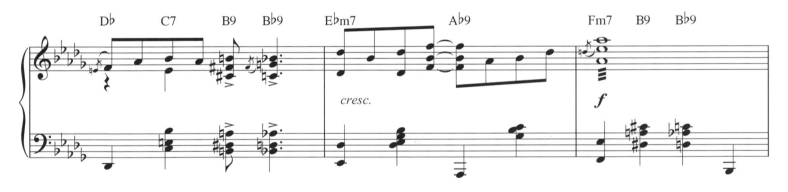

Double-time feel, Swing 16ths

46

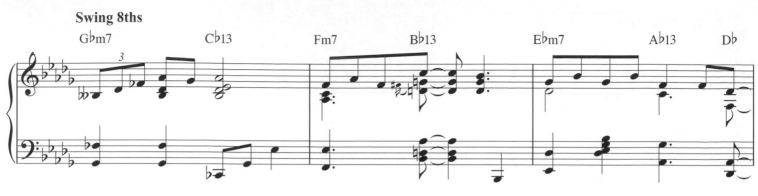

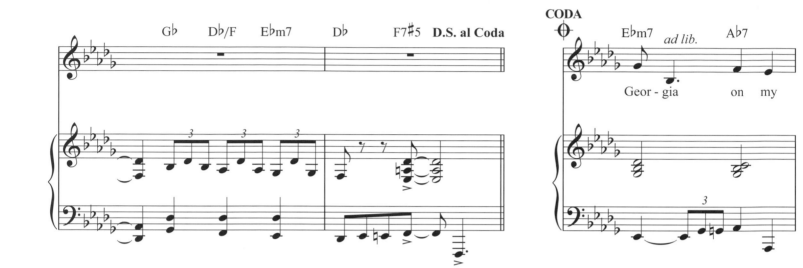

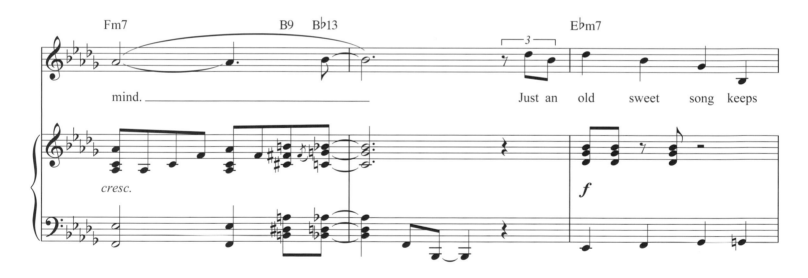

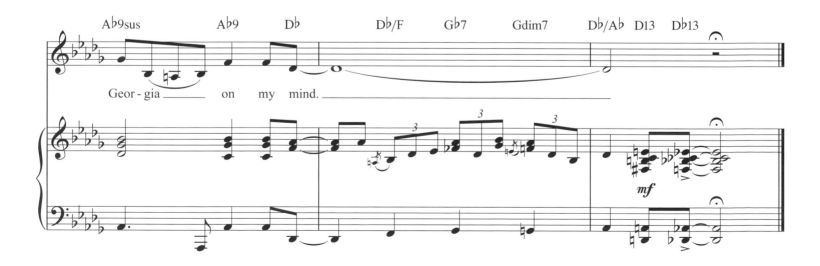

I CAN'T GET STARTED
from ZIEGFELD FOLLIES

Words by IRA GERSHWIN
Music by VERNON DUKE

I've flown a - round the world_ in a plane.___ I've set - tled
hun - dred yards_ in ten flat.___ The Prince of

rev - o - lu - tions in Spain. The North Pole I have chart - ed, but
Wales has cop - ied my hat. With queens I've à la cart - ed, but

can't get start - ed with you.___ A - round a
can't get start - ed with you.___ The lead - ing

HONEYSUCKLE ROSE

from AIN'T MISBEHAVIN'
from TIN PAN ALLEY

Words by ANDY RAZAF
Music by THOMAS "FATS" WALLER

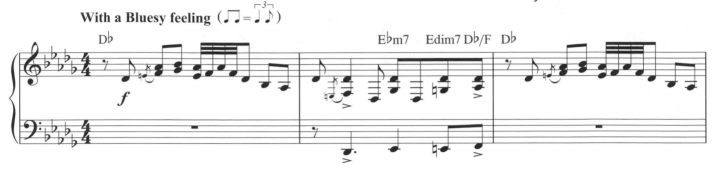

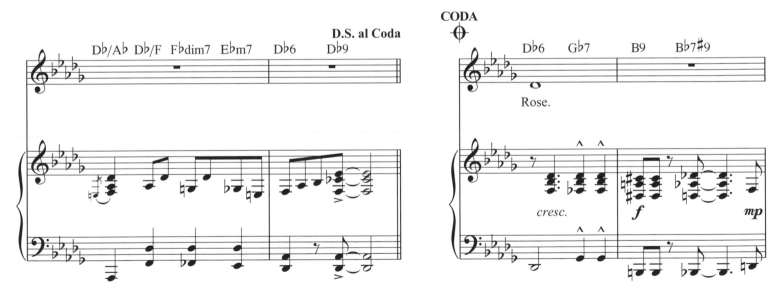

HOW HIGH THE MOON

from TWO FOR THE SHOW

Lyrics by NANCY HAMILTON
Music by MORGAN LEWIS

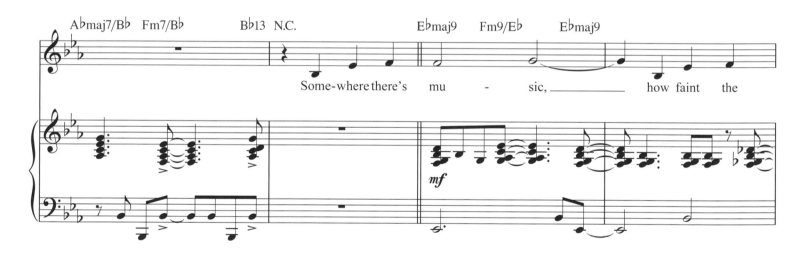

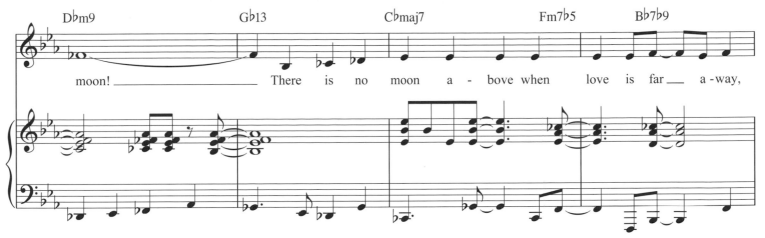

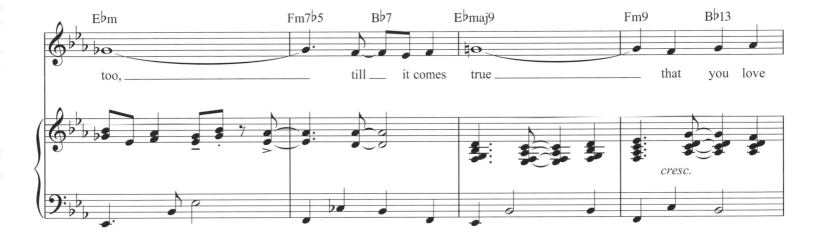

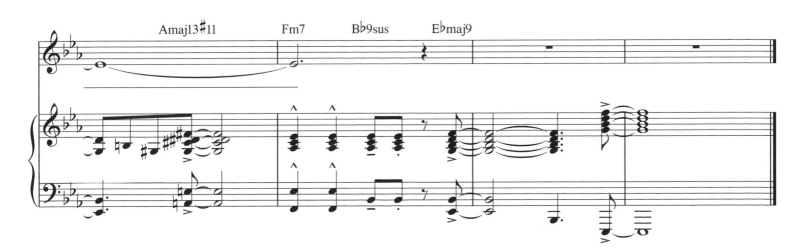

IT MIGHT AS WELL BE SPRING

from STATE FAIR

Lyrics by OSCAR HAMMERSTEIN II
Music by RICHARD RODGERS

60

IT'S ONLY A PAPER MOON

Lyric by BILLY ROSE and E.Y. "YIP" HARBURG
Music by HAROLD ARLEN

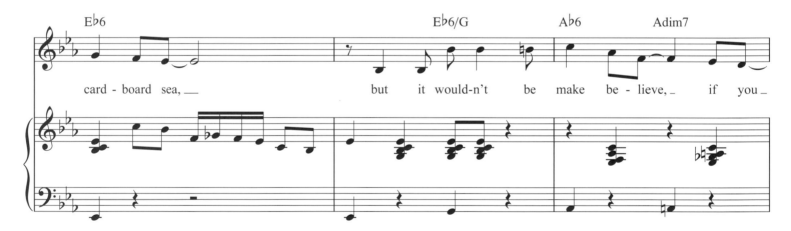

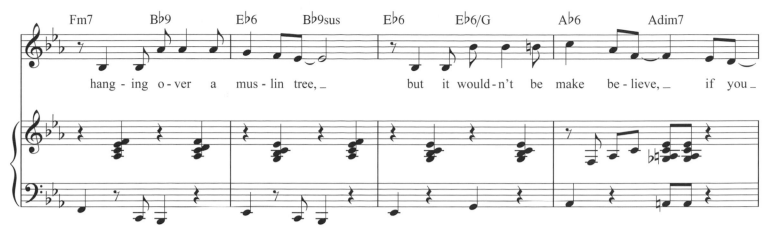

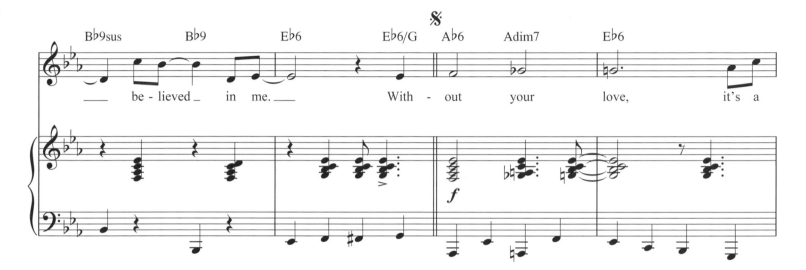

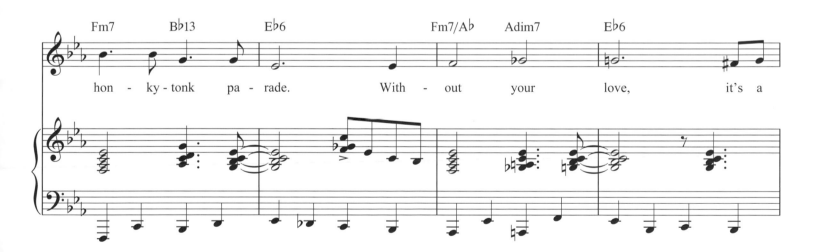

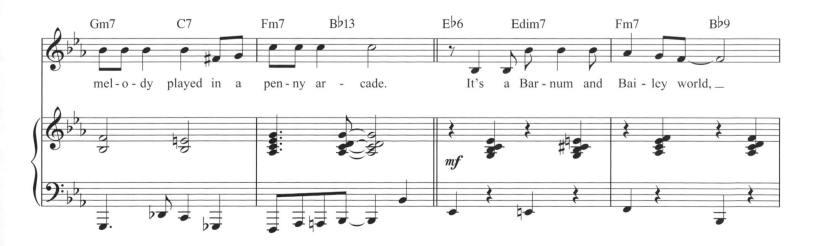

just as pho-ny as it can be, ___ But it would-n't be make be-lieve, ___ if you ___

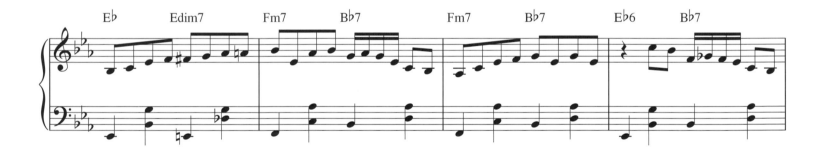

be-lieved ___ in me. ___ With- ___ be-lieved ___ in me. ___

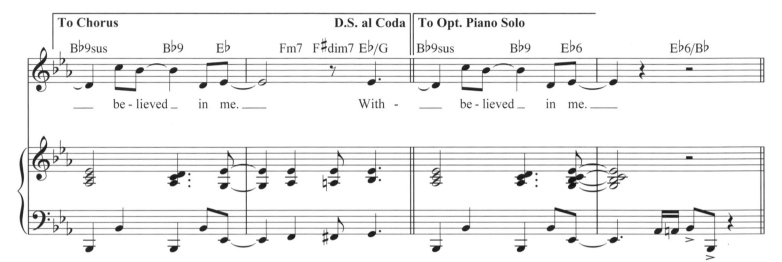

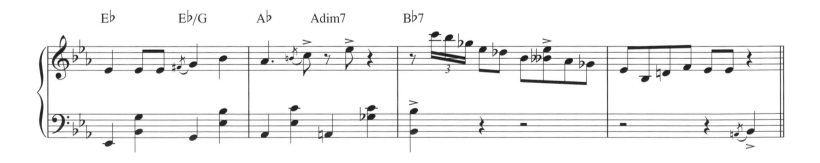

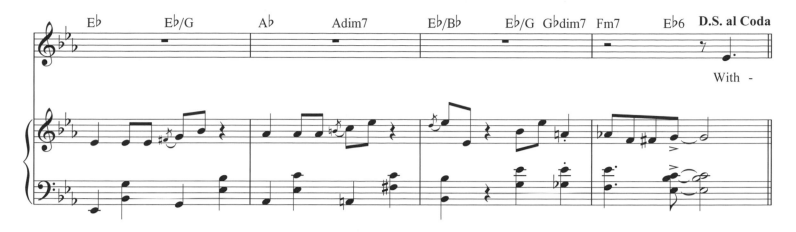

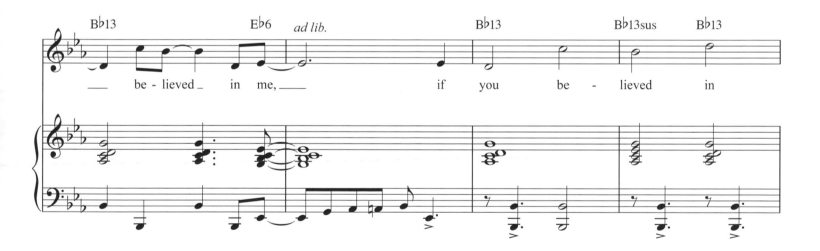

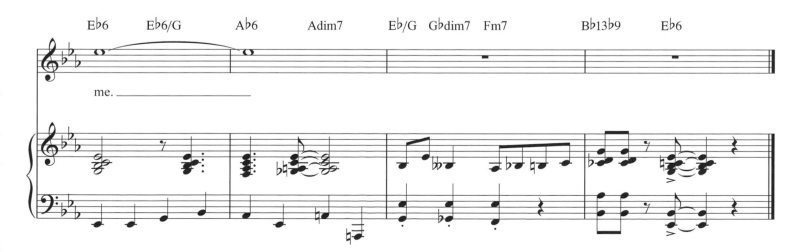

MISTY

Words by JOHNNY BURKE
Music by ERROLL GARNER

68

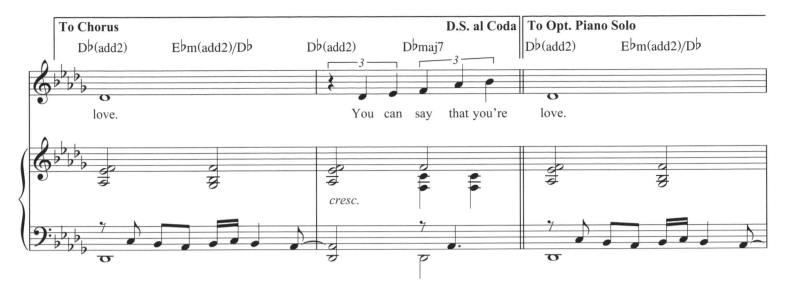

To Chorus

D.S. al Coda

To Opt. Piano Solo

love.

You can say that you're

love.

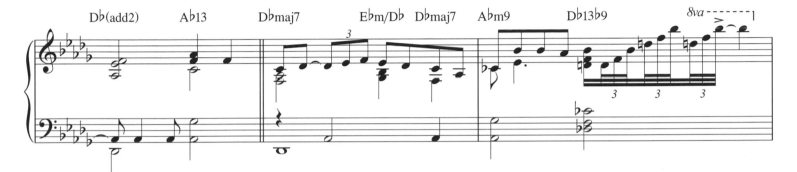

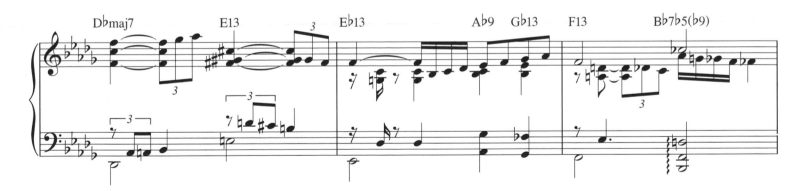

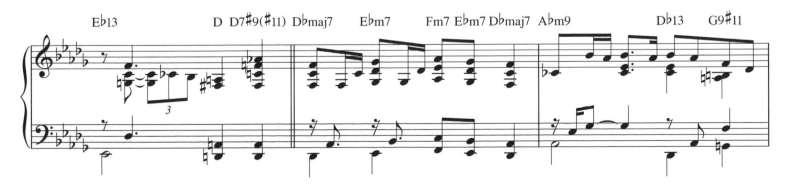

ROUTE 66

By BOBBY TROUP

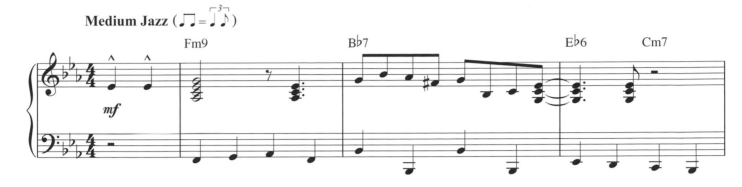

If you ev - er _____ plan to mo - tor west, ___

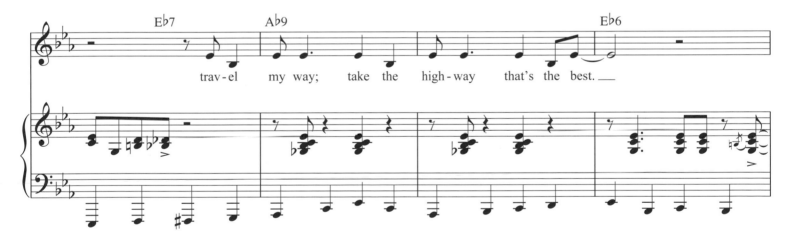

trav - el my way; take the high - way that's the best. ___

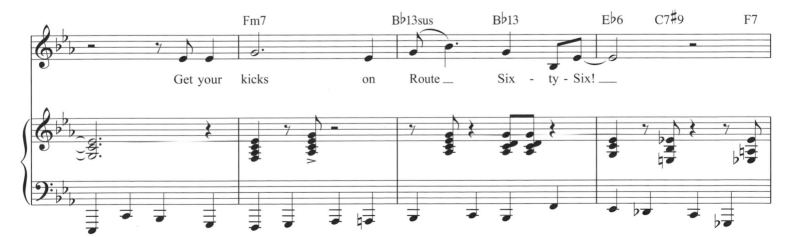

Get your kicks on Route _____ Six - ty - Six! ___

72

It winds _____ from Chi - ca - go to L. A., _____

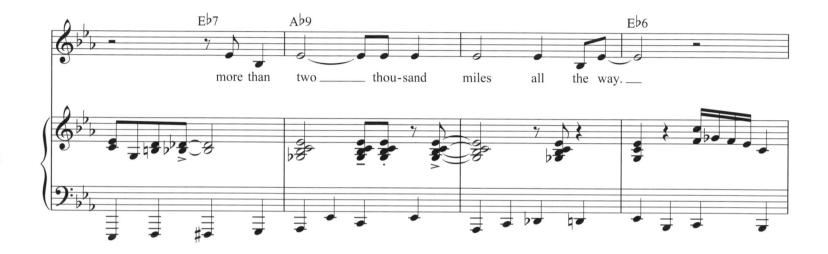

more than two _____ thou-sand miles all the way. _____

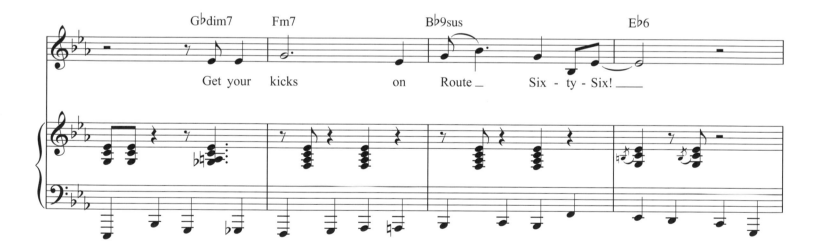

Get your kicks on Route _ Six - ty - Six! _____

Now you go thru Saint Loo - ey, Jop - lin, Mis - sou - ri; and

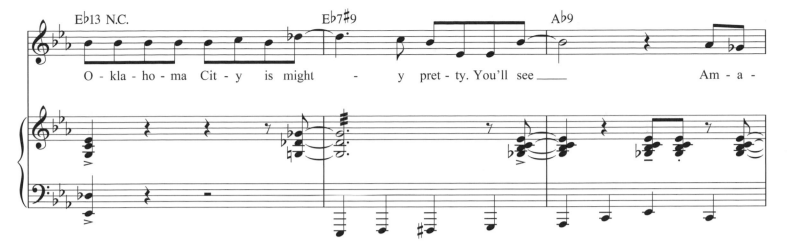

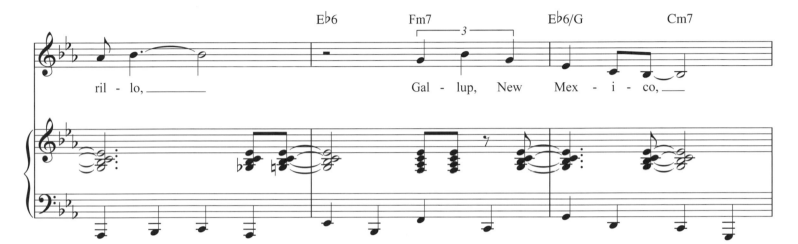

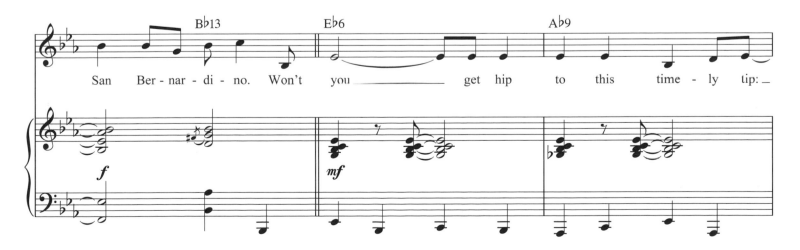

When you ___ make that Cal - i - for - nia trip, ___

get your kicks on Route ___ Six - ty - Six! ___

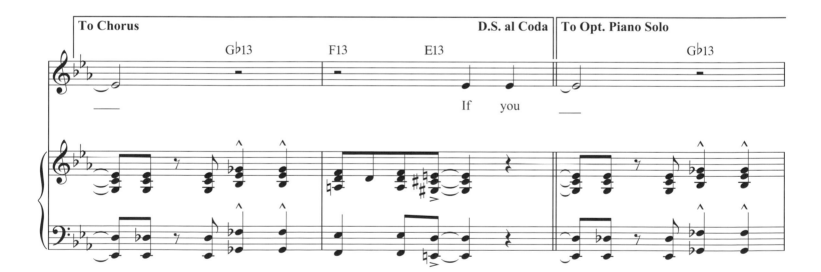

If you ___

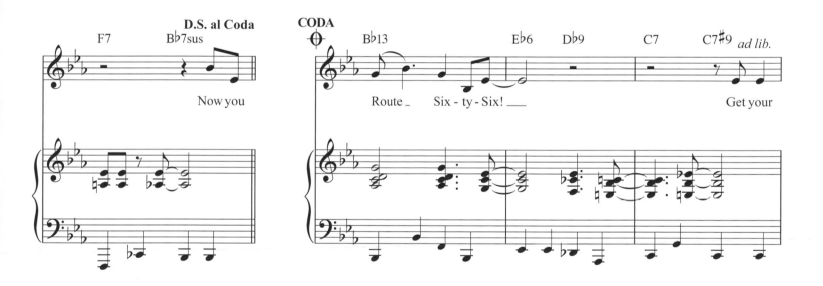

MY ROMANCE
from JUMBO

Words by LORENZ HART
Music by RICHARD RODGERS

Easy Swing

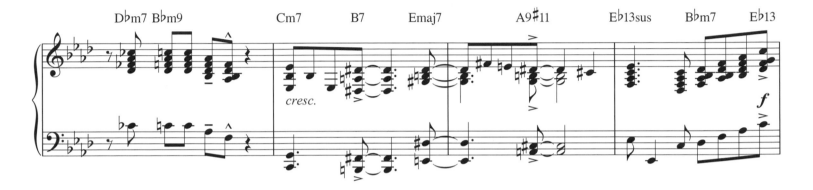

My ro - mance does-n't have to have a moon in the

sky, my ro - mance does-n't need a blue la - goon stand - ing

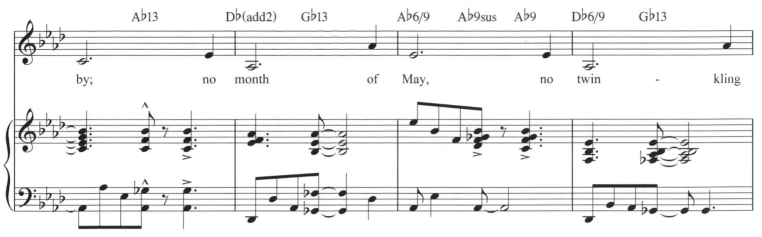

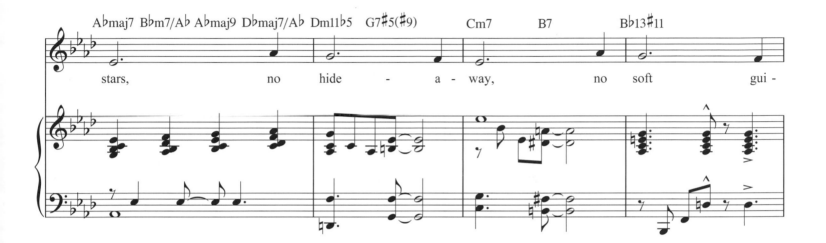

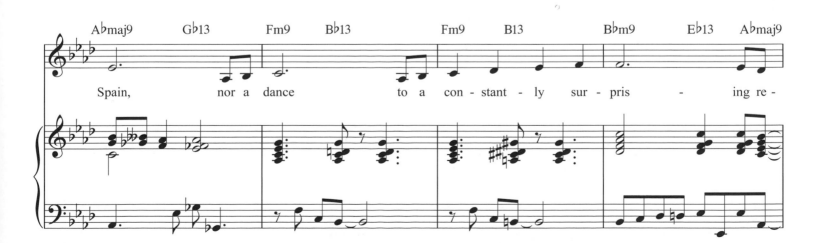

Ebm9 Ab9 Dbmaj7 F7#5(b9) Bbm7 Gm11b5 Gb7#11 Fm7

frain. Wide a - wake I can make my most fan - tas - tic dreams come

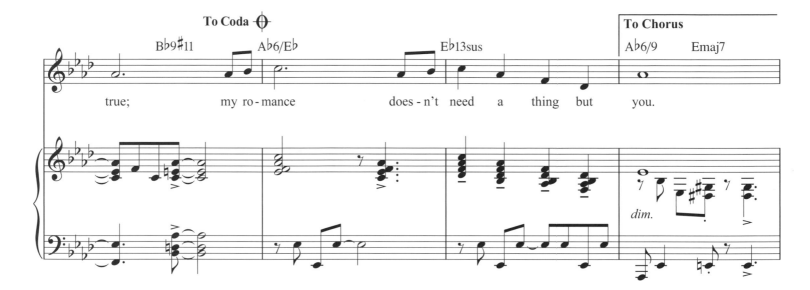

To Coda

Bb9#11 Ab6/Eb Eb13sus **To Chorus** Ab6/9 Emaj7

true; my ro - mance does - n't need a thing but you.

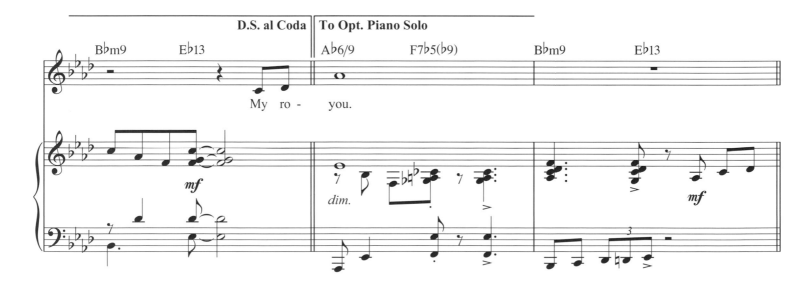

D.S. al Coda | **To Opt. Piano Solo**

Bbm9 Eb13 Ab6/9 F7b5(b9) Bbm9 Eb13

My ro - you.

Ab6/9 Bbm9 Cm7 F7#5 Bbm9 Eb13 Abmaj9 Gb13

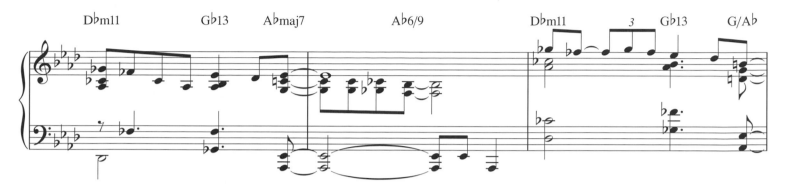

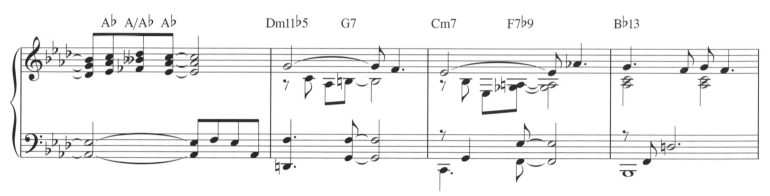

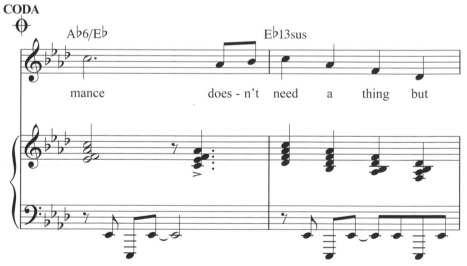

My ro- mance does-n't need a thing but

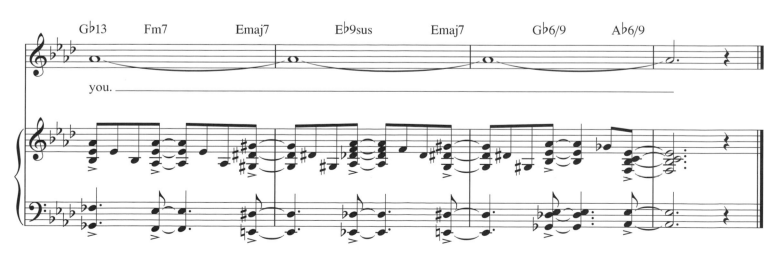

you.

THE NEARNESS OF YOU
from the Paramount Picture ROMANCE IN THE DARK

Words by NED WASHINGTON
Music by HOAGY CARMICHAEL

I need no soft lights to en-chant me if

you'll on-ly grant me the right ____ to hold you ev-er so

To Coda

tight, ____ and to feel in the night the near-ness of

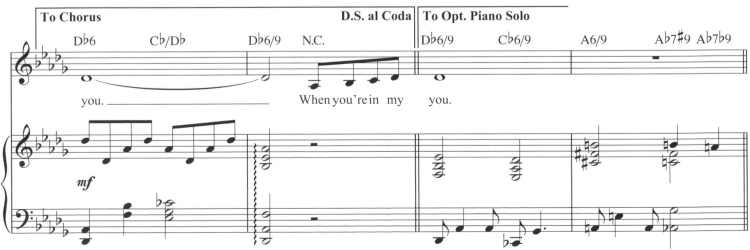

To Chorus   **D.S. al Coda**   **To Opt. Piano Solo**

you. ____ When you're in my you.

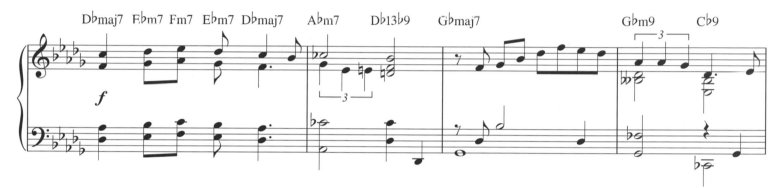

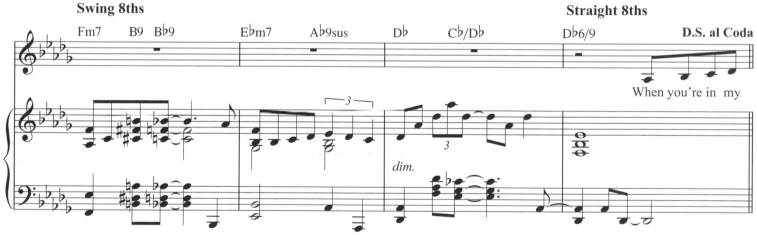

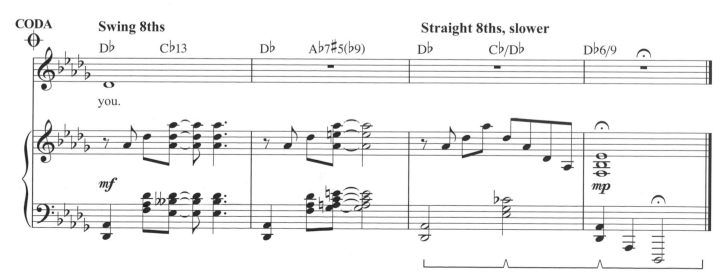

SOME OTHER TIME

from ON THE TOWN

Lyrics by BETTY COMDEN
and ADOLPH GREEN
Music by LEONARD BERNSTEIN

time is rac - ing. Oh, well, we'll catch up Some oth-er time. _____

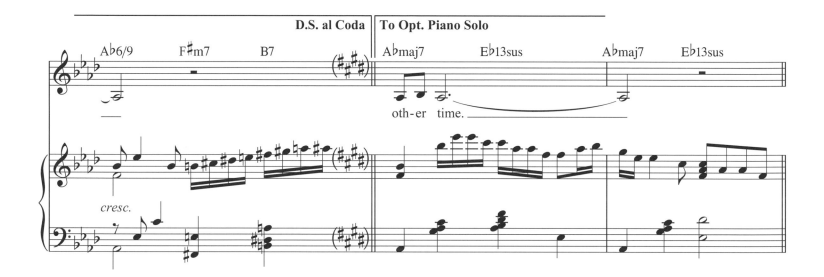

oth-er time. _____

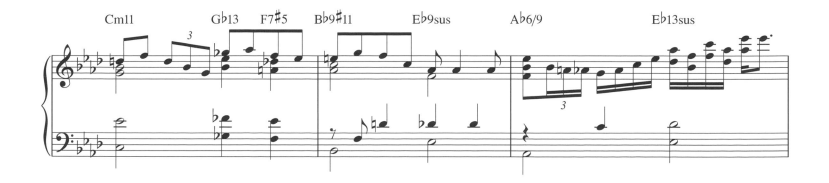

STARDUST

Words by MITCHELL PARISH
Music by HOAGY CARMICHAEL

far a-way, leav-ing me a song that will not die.

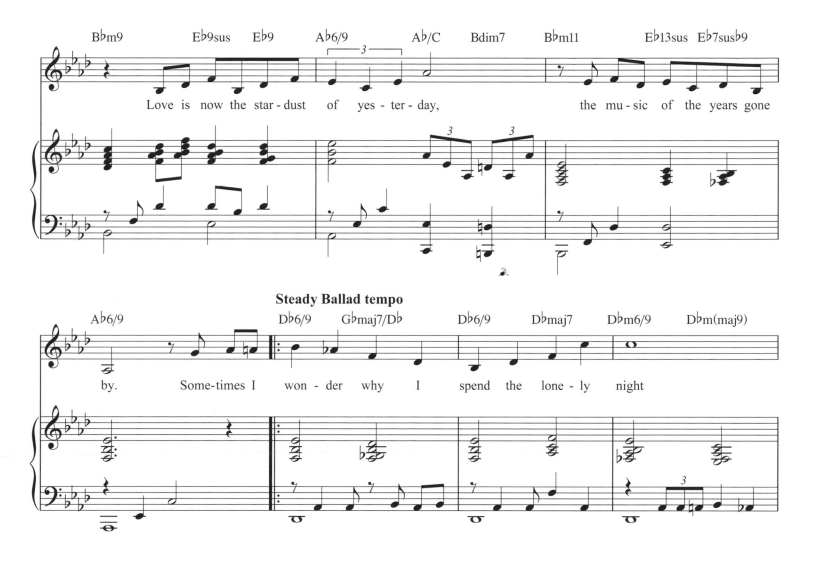

Love is now the star-dust of yes-ter-day, the mu-sic of the years gone

Steady Ballad tempo

by. Some-times I won-der why I spend the lone-ly night

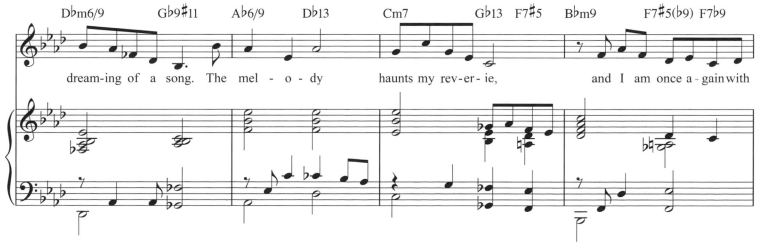

dream-ing of a song. The mel-o-dy haunts my rev-er-ie, and I am once a-gain with

you, _____ when our love was new, and each kiss an in-spi-ra - tion. _____

_____ But that was long a - go: now my con-so-la - tion is

Lilting Swing

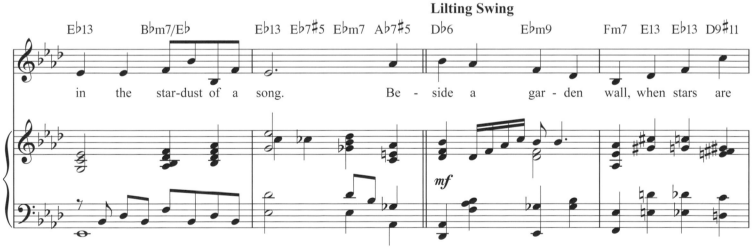

in the star-dust of a song. Be - side a gar - den wall, when stars are

bright, you are in my arms. The night - in - gale tells his fair - y tale

(There Is)
NO GREATER LOVE

Words by MARTY SYMES
Music by ISHAM JONES

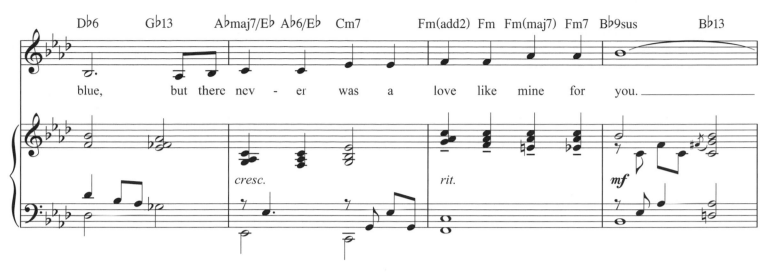

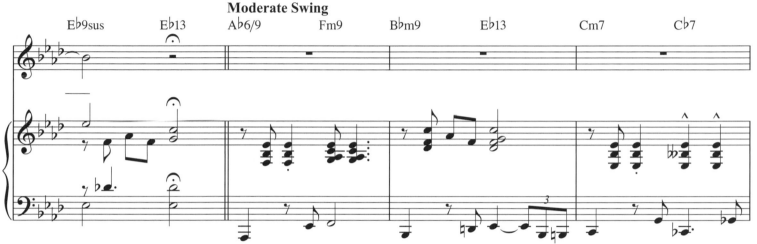

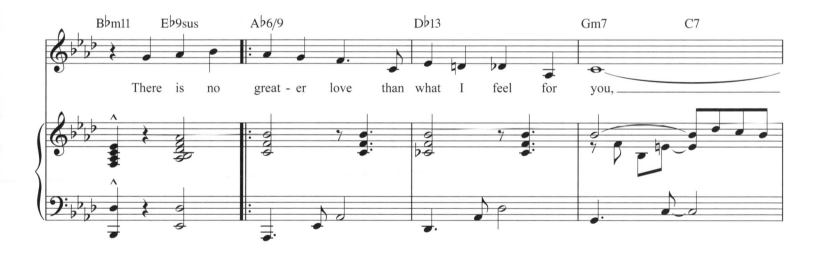

There is no great-er thrill than what you bring to me,

no sweet-er song than what you sing to me.

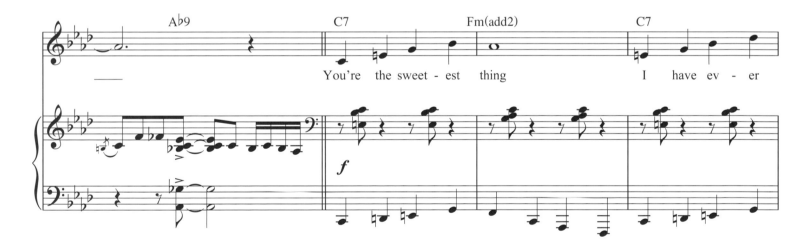

You're the sweet-est thing I have ev-er

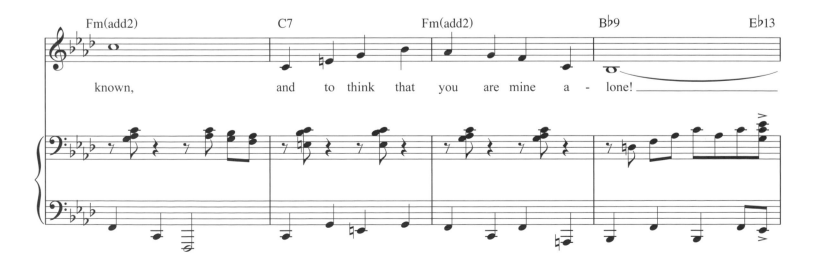

known, and to think that you are mine a-lone!

THE VERY THOUGHT OF YOU

Words and Music by
RAY NOBLE

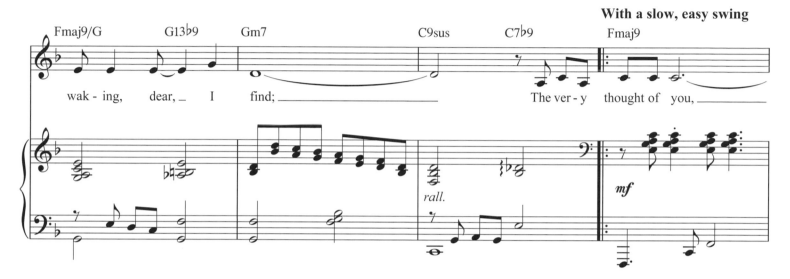

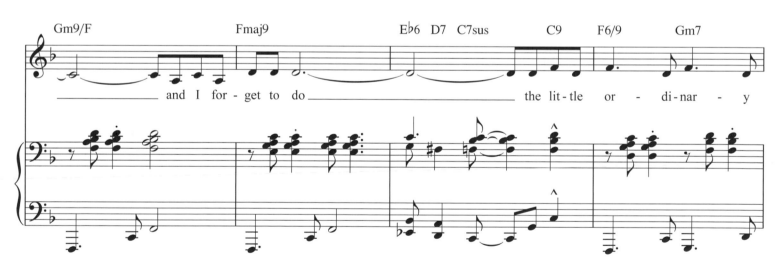

98

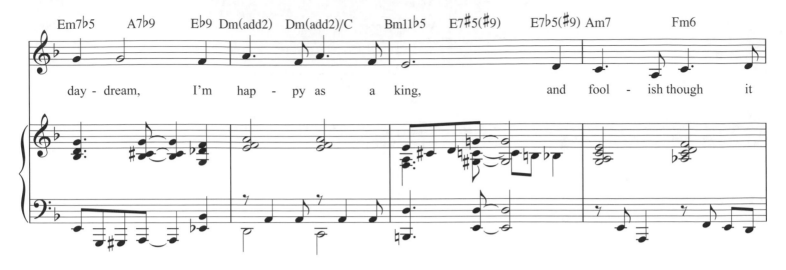

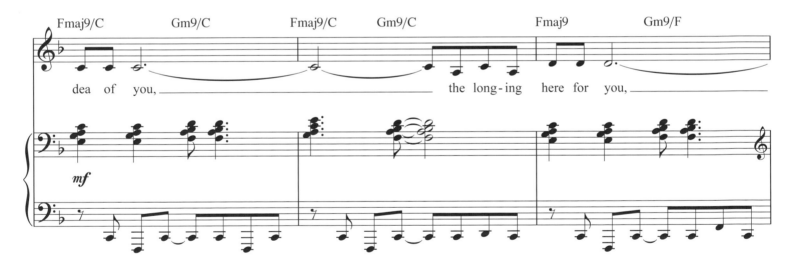

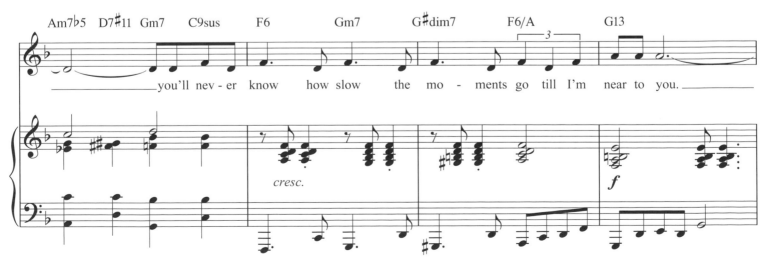

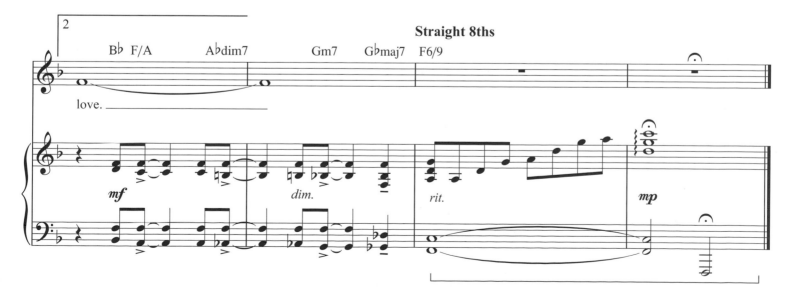

WHEN I FALL IN LOVE

from ONE MINUTE TO ZERO

Words by EDWARD HEYMAN
Music by VICTOR YOUNG

Slow Swing, with much feeling

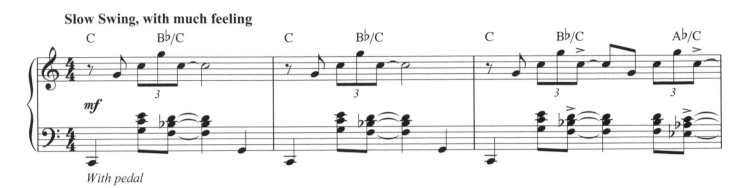

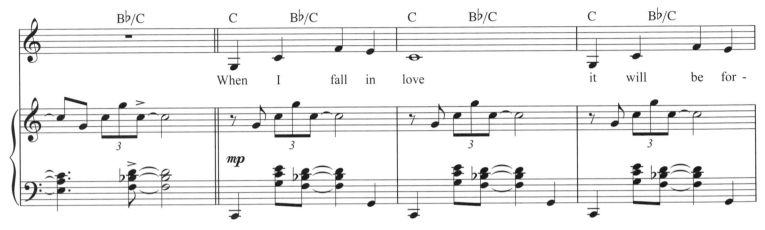

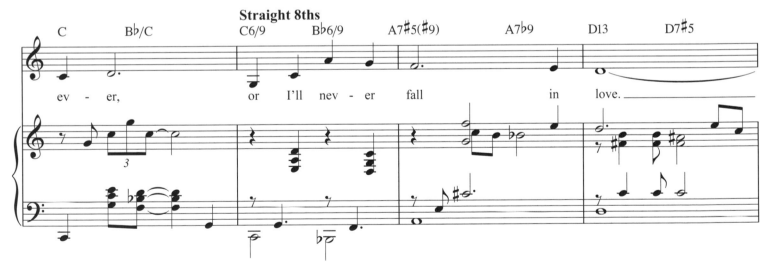

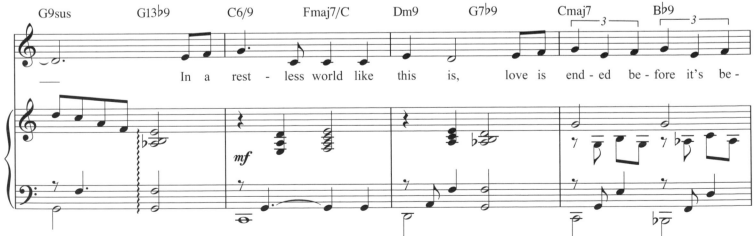

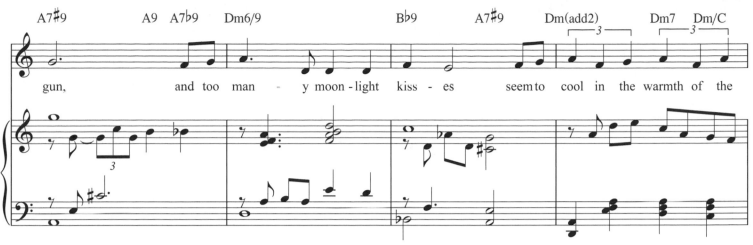

gun,　　　and too man - y moon - light kiss - es　seem to cool in the warmth of the

sun.　　　When I give my heart　　　it will be com -

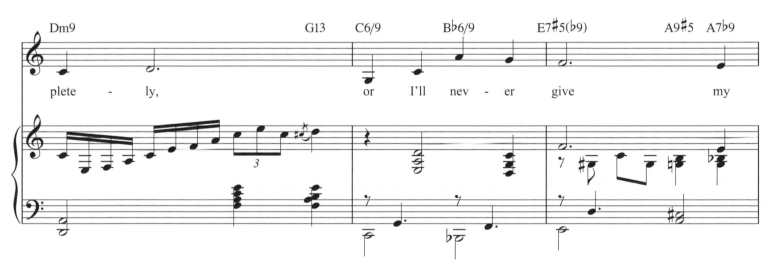

plete - ly,　　　or I'll nev - er give　　　my

heart. _____　　And the mo - ment I can　feel that　you

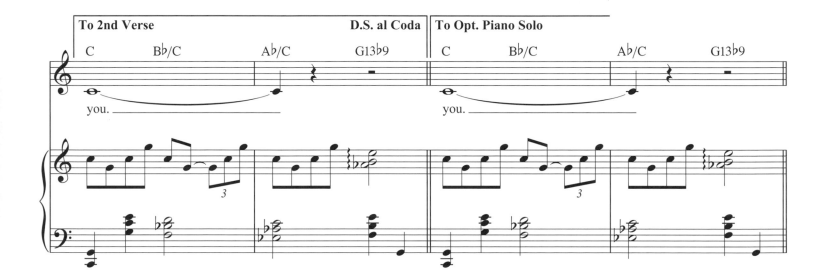

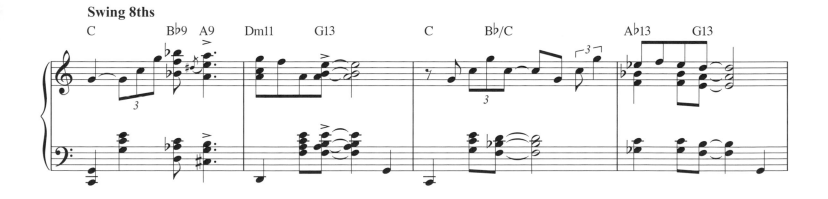

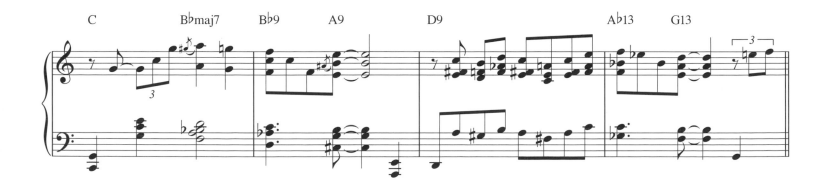

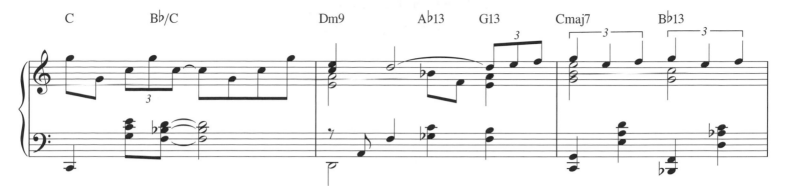

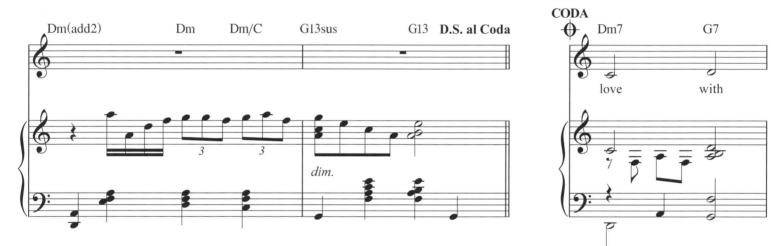

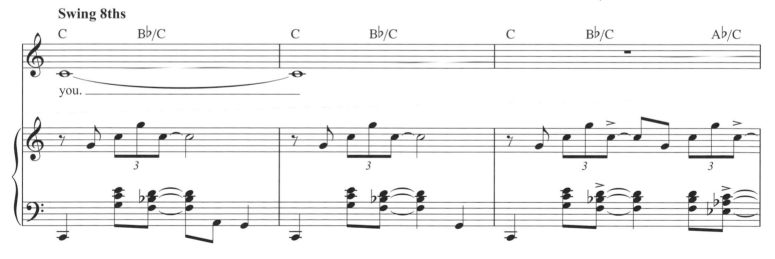

TENDERLY
from TORCH SONG

Lyric by JACK LAWRENCE
Music by WALTER GROSS

Moderate Swing

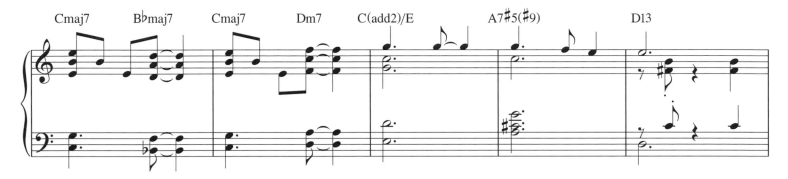

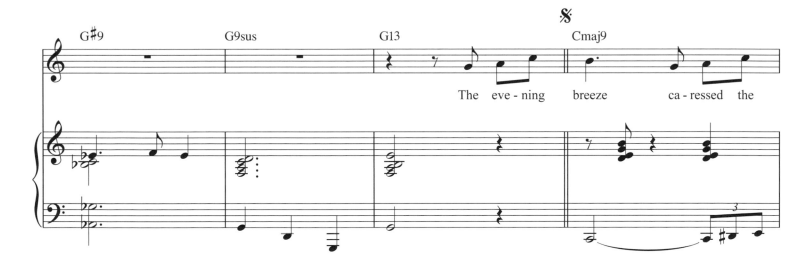

The eve-ning breeze ca-ressed the

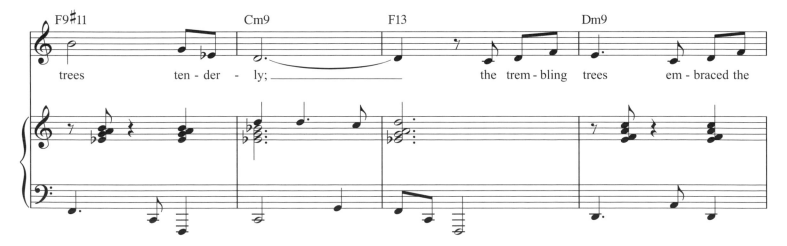

trees ten-der-ly; _____ the trem-bling trees em-braced the

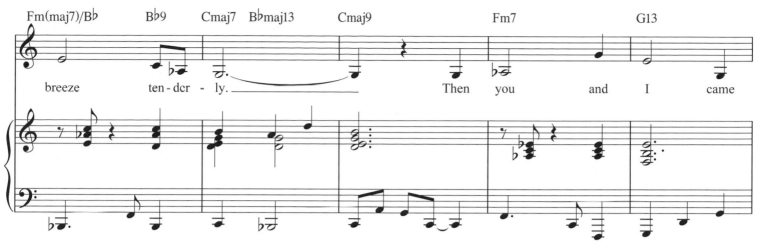

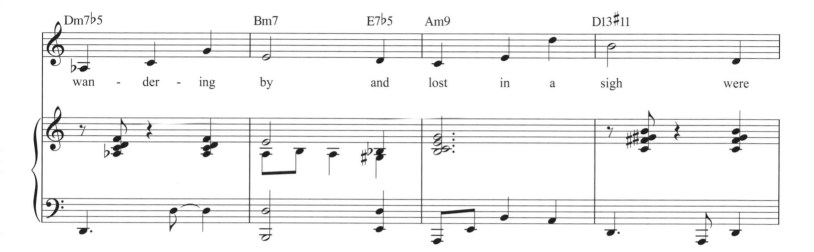

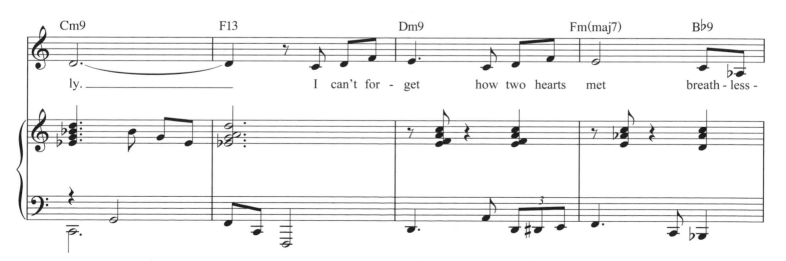

Your arms o - pened wide and

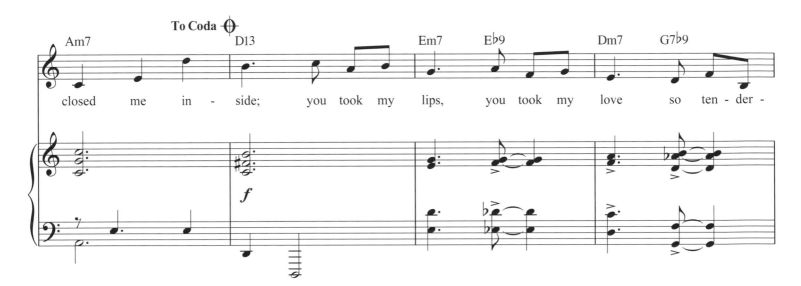

closed me in - side; you took my lips, you took my love so ten - der -

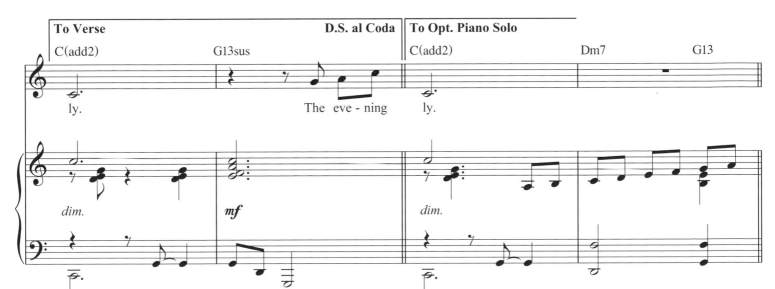

ly. The eve - ning ly.

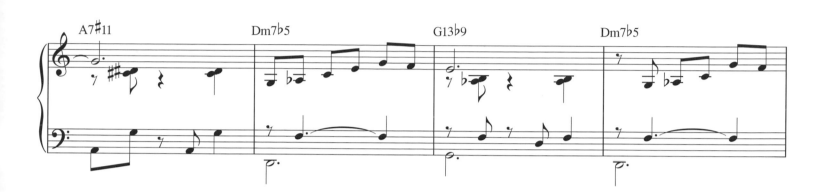

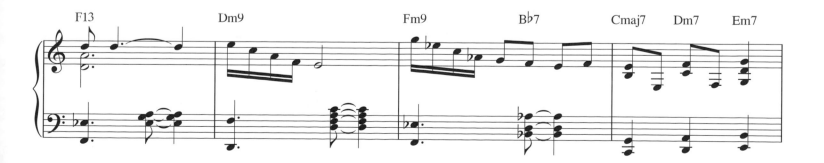

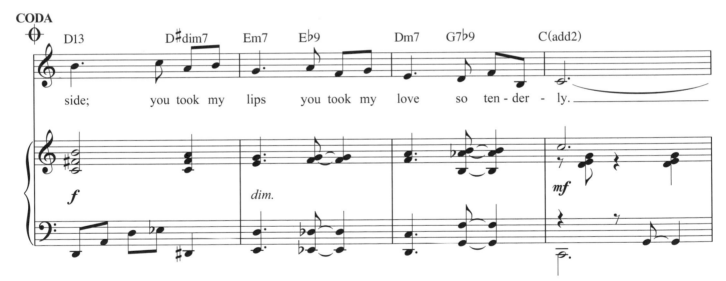

Freely, straight 8ths

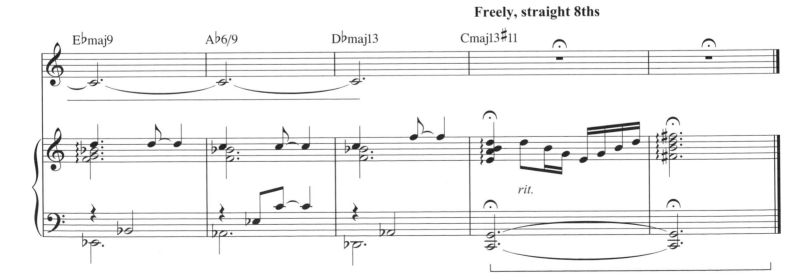